KU-288-749

ISLINGTON LIBRARIES

3 0120 02826779 7

THE AUSTRALIAN Women's Weekly

BAKING

THE AUSTRALIAN Women's Weekly

BAKING

BREADS, CAKES, BISCUITS, AND BAKES

Project Editor Emma Hill
Project Designer Alison Shackleton
Editorial Assistant Kiron Gill
Jacket Designer Alison Donovan
Jackets Coordinator Lucy Philpott
Production Editor Heather Blagden
Senior Producer Luca Bazzoli
Creative Technical Support Sonia Charbonnier
Managing Editor Dawn Henderson
Managing Art Editor Alison Donovan
Art Director Maxine Pedliham
Publishing Director Katie Cowan

First published in Great Britain in 2021
by Dorling Kindersley Limited
DK, One Embassy Gardens, 8 Viaduct Gardens, London, SW11 7BW

The authorised representative in the EEA is Dorling Kindersley
Verlag GmbH. Arnulfstr. 124, 80636 Munich, Germany

Copyright © 2021 Dorling Kindersley Limited
A Penguin Random House Company
10 9 8 7 6 5 4 3 2 1
001–324524–Aug/2021

All rights reserved.
No part of this publication may be reproduced, stored in or introduced into
a retrieval system, or transmitted, in any form, or by any means (electronic,
mechanical, photocopying, recording, or otherwise), without the prior
written permission of the copyright owner.

A CIP catalogue record for this book is available from the British Library.
ISBN: 978-0-2415-1016-2

Printed and bound in China

For the curious
www.dk.com

MIX
Paper from
responsible sources
FSC™ C018179

This book was made with Forest Stewardship Council ™ certified paper –
one small step in DK's commitment to a sustainable future.
For more information go to **www.dk.com/our-green-pledge**

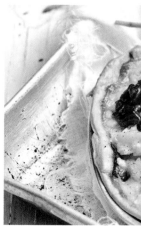

Contents

Introduction   6

Biscuits and slices   **8**

Cakes and cupcakes   **44**

Pies and tarts   **92**

Breads, scones, and scrolls   **154**

Conversion chart   188

Index   189

Acknowledgments   192

Baking essentials

No matter what your skill level, this practical and beautiful book contains sweet and savoury recipes for all your essential baking needs. Along the way there are plenty of tips and twists to help you master the basics and hone your skills.

Getting started

There is a delicate balance between ingredients and a multitude of chemical reactions with even the most basic of bakes. For successful baking it is important to use the stated ingredients, accurately measure both dry and liquid ingredients, and use the correct sized eggs (we use large 60g eggs). Precision is critical – a little more of something, or a little less, can throw a recipe out, so use scales to get your measurements just right. Levelling ingredients when measuring in a cup or spoon is a key step when measuring dry ingredients. Fill the cup or spoon then gently shake it so the ingredients sit level to the top before levelling with a knife or spatula.

Spray measuring spoons with a little cooking oil when measuring sticky ingredients such as honey or golden syrup – this will prevent the ingredient from sticking to the spoon and will give you a more accurate measure. Don't forget to level the spoon – more is not always better. Measure liquids in a marked jug by standing the jug on a flat surface and checking the amount at eye level. Many measuring jugs have both imperial and metric measures marked on them so take care to look at the right units for your bake.

Butter and eggs

Cold ingredients such as butter and eggs are best brought to room temperature before baking cakes. Place eggs in a bowl of warm water for 5–10 minutes to bring them up to room temperature. To soften butter quickly, coarsely chop or grate it into a bowl and stand over hot water for a few minutes, or microwave for 5 seconds at a time until the butter is just soft. When separating eggs, use a separate bowl and crack them one at a time – this way if you break a yolk, it won't fall into the whole bowl of whites. Use egg shell to scoop out any small bits of yolk from the whites as the fat from the yolk will inhibit aeration.

How to store cakes

Most cakes keep well for 2 or 3 days – as a rule, the higher the fat content the longer a cake will keep. Store cakes in an airtight container as close to the cake size as possible to minimize the airspace around the cake. Make sure the cake has cooled to room temperature before putting it in the container. Many cakes also freeze well – this is best done before they are filled or iced. You can thaw whole cakes overnight in the refrigerator, while slices need only 10–15 minutes at room temperature to thaw.

Equipment

Here is a list of equipment that you will find useful to have in your kitchen, ready for baking. Build your collection as your interest and expertise grow:

MEASURING CUPS For dry ingredients you'll need Australian standard metric measuring cups graduating from 1/4 cup (60ml) to 1 cup (250ml). See page 188 for more information on how to use Australian measures.

MEASURING SPOONS Australia is the only country in the world to have a metric 20ml tablespoon – other countries use an imperial 15ml (3 teaspoons) tablespoon. Check yours are metric. See page 188 for more information on how to use the measures in this book.

MEASURING JUGS Choose a clear plastic or glass jug for ease of use. The most useful are the 1-litre and 250ml sizes.

SCALES Electric scales are best so you can return the display to zero (tare) after you position the bowl on them for ingredients.

MIXING BOWLS You'll need a variety of sizes and shapes. Use wide bowls for mixing ingredients with a spoon or whisk, and tall, deep bowls with an electric mixer when volume is created. Stainless steel bowls are non-reactive and heatproof while ceramic or heatproof glass bowls are microwave safe. You will need a heatproof bowl to fit over a saucepan to make a double boiler (bain-marie) for melting chocolate.

SPOONS AND SPATULAS Large metal spoons are used to fold ingredients together, while wooden spoons are for creaming and stirring. Wood absorbs flavours and fat so keep separate spoons for sweet and savoury cooking. Rubber and plastic spatulas are used for scraping down bowls – you will need a large and small one, and they should be flexible and moulded in one piece.

WHISKS Balloon whisks are used for whisking cream or egg whites and folding mixtures. For ease of use, choose a large version with flexible wires. Small, stiff whisks are usually used for mixing when aeration is not a requirement.

SIEVES We recommend having nylon and metal sieves in small, medium, and large sizes.

PALETTE KNIVES A long palette knife is particularly handy for icing cakes and sliding under cakes or cookies when lifting. Short, straight, or cranked palette knives are used for spreading icing, fillings, and mixtures into pans, and also for lifting cookies from oven trays.

GRATERS For grating citrus rind and ginger, we recommend using a microplane grater.

ROLLING PINS Choose from marble, wood, or glass; all are suitable choices for baking.

PASTRY BRUSHES We recommend brushes made from natural fibres or silicon.

WIRE COOLING RACKS Rectangular shapes tend to be the most useful. Finer racks are better to minimize damage to small or delicate baked items.

BISCUITS AND SLICES

From classic buttery biscuits and the chewiest of cookies to delectable slices, here you'll find an array of sweet treats perfect for sharing as a small yet satisfying snack.

Chocolate chip cookies

PREP + COOK TIME **30 MINUTES** | MAKES **44**

Make the humble classic chocolate chip cookie here, or try one of the delicious flavour variations on pages 12–13. Keep in mind that a shorter cooking time will result in a chewier texture.

250g butter, softened

1 tsp vanilla extract

3/4 cup (165g) caster sugar

3/4 cup (165g) firmly packed brown sugar

1 egg

2 1/4 cups (335g) plain flour

1 tsp bicarbonate of soda

375g dark chocolate, coarsely chopped

1 Preheat oven to 180°C (160°C fan/350°F/Gas 4). Grease three oven trays; line with baking paper.

2 Beat the butter, vanilla, sugars, and egg in a small bowl with an electric mixer until light and fluffy. Transfer the mixture to a large bowl; stir in the sifted flour and bicarbonate of soda, in two batches. Stir in the chocolate.

3 Roll tablespoons of the mixture into balls; place on the oven trays about 5cm apart.

4 Bake the cookies for 12 minutes for a chewier cookie or for 14 minutes for a crispier texture, removing when golden and crisp. Cool on trays.

TIP

Chocolate chip cookies will keep in an airtight container for up to 1 week.

Chocolate chip cookie variations

For these cookies, make the chocolate chip cookies on page 11 omitting, swapping, and adding ingredients as directed in the individual recipes below to bring in your favourite flavours and textures.

Oats and sultanas

TOP LEFT Make the chocolate chip cookies on page 11, adding $1/4$ cup (40g) sultanas and 2 tablespoons of rolled oats with the chocolate in step 2. Continue as directed in the recipe.

White choc and macadamia

TOP RIGHT Make the chocolate chip cookies on page 11, omitting the chopped chocolate. Add $3/4$ cup (105g) coarsely chopped raw macadamias and 200g coarsely chopped good-quality white chocolate to the cookie dough at the end of step 2. Continue as directed in the recipe.

Peanut butter cup

BOTTOM MIDDLE Make the chocolate chip cookies on page 11, omitting the chopped chocolate. Add 2 x 42g bars chopped Reese's Milk Chocolate Peanut Butter Cups, 200g chopped milk chocolate, and $1/2$ cup (70g) chopped roasted peanuts to the cookie dough at the end of step 2. Continue as directed in the recipe.

Triple chocolate

TOP MIDDLE Make the chocolate chip cookies on page 11, omitting the chopped chocolate. Stir in 125g each of white, milk, and dark chopped chocolate to the cookie dough at the end of step 2. Continue as directed in the recipe.

Hazelnut and dark choc

BOTTOM LEFT Make the chocolate chip cookies on page 11, adding only 200g chopped dark chocolate. Add $3/4$ cup (105g) chopped roasted skinless hazelnuts to the cookie dough at the end of step 2. Continue as directed in the recipe.

Rich chocolate chip

BOTTOM RIGHT Make the chocolate chip cookies on page 11, reducing the plain flour to 2 cups (300g). Add $1/4$ cup (25g) cocoa powder to the flour and bicarbonate of soda before sifting in step 2. Continue as directed in the recipe.

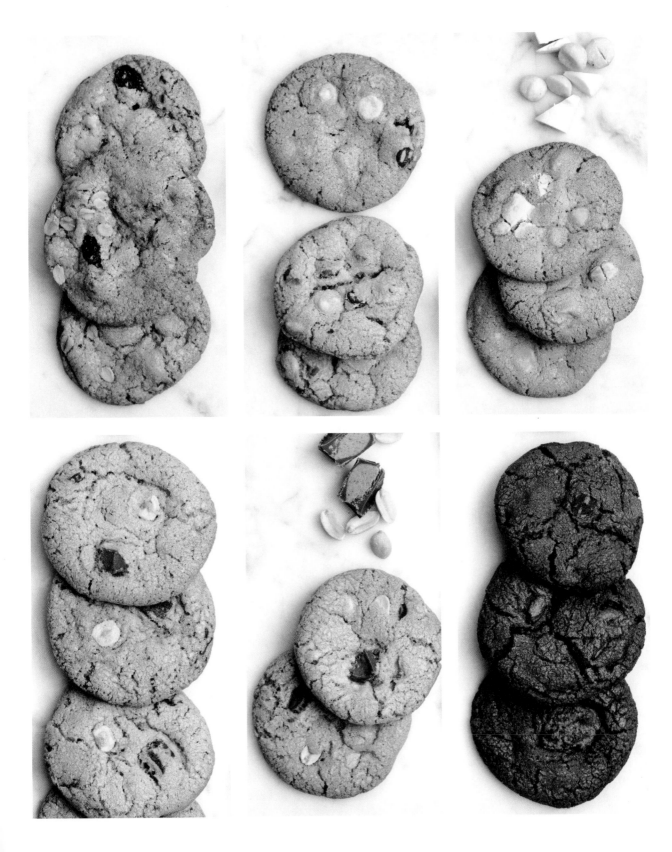

5-ingredient triple chocolate brownies

PREP + COOK TIME **40 MINUTES** | MAKES **12**

Pure indulgence for chocolate lovers, these irresistible triple chocolate brownies are so simple to make, and only five ingredients are needed. If you like a gooey centre, be extra careful not to over-bake.

4 eggs, at room temperature

220g chocolate hazelnut spread

1/4 cup (45g) milk chocolate chips

1/4 cup (45g) white chocolate chips

2 tsp cocoa powder

1 Preheat oven to 180°C (160°C fan/350°F/Gas 4). Grease a 20cm square cake pan; line the bottom and sides with baking paper, extending the paper 5cm over the edges.

2 Beat the eggs in a medium bowl with an electric mixer on high speed for 10 minutes or until tripled in volume.

3 Meanwhile, place the chocolate hazelnut spread in a large microwave-safe bowl; microwave on HIGH for 20 seconds or until softened slightly.

4 Fold the egg mixture into the chocolate hazelnut mixture, in three batches. Pour the mixture into the cake pan.

5 Bake the brownie for 20 minutes. Remove from the oven; sprinkle with the combined chocolate chips. Bake for a further 5 minutes or until a skewer inserted into centre comes out clean. Cool in the pan.

6 Lift the brownie from the pan; dust with the cocoa powder, then cut into 12 pieces to serve.

TIP

Brownies will keep at room temperature, in an airtight container, for up to 3 days.

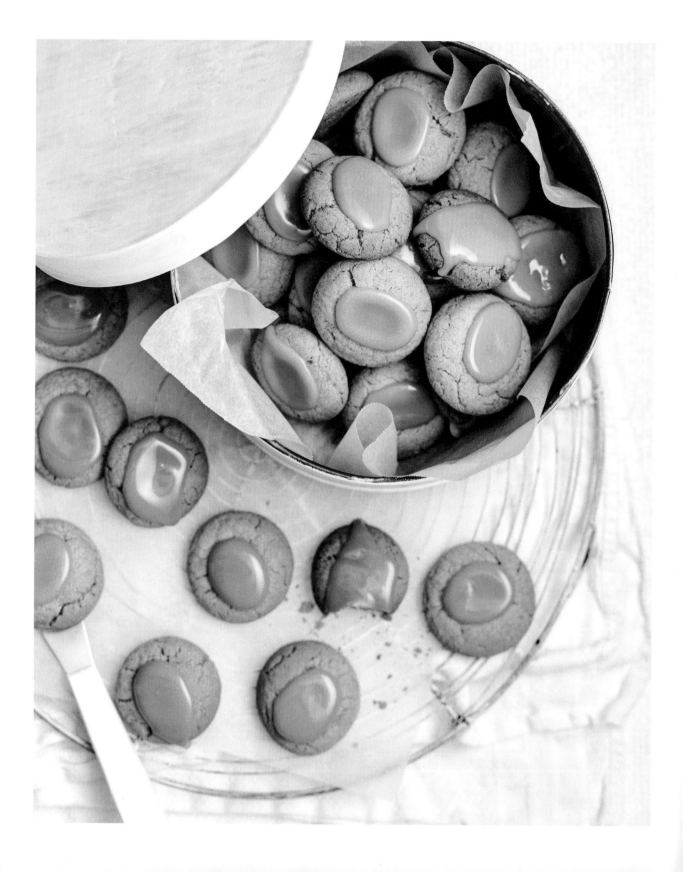

Caramel ginger crunchies

PREP + COOK TIME **1 HOUR** | MAKES **45**

These crunchies will fill your kitchen with the warm aromas of ginger and cinnamon, while a dollop of indulgent caramel brings added richness to the classic ginger biscuit. Best enjoyed straight out of the oven for full appreciation of their gooey gorgeousness.

2 cups (300g) plain flour

1/2 tsp bicarbonate of soda

1 tsp ground cinnamon

2 tsp ground ginger

1 cup (220g) caster sugar

125g cold butter, chopped

1 egg

1 tsp golden syrup or treacle

2 tbsp finely chopped glacé ginger

45 wrapped hard caramels

1   Preheat oven to 180°C (160°C fan/350°F/Gas 4). Grease two large oven trays; line with baking paper.

2   Process the sifted dry ingredients with the butter until the mixture is crumbly. Add the egg, golden syrup, and glacé ginger; process until the ingredients come together. Knead the dough on a floured surface until smooth.

3   Roll well-rounded teaspoons of the mixture into balls; place them 3cm apart on the oven trays.

4   Bake the biscuits for 12 minutes. Place a caramel on top of each hot biscuit; bake for a further 5 minutes or until the caramel begins to melt. Cool the biscuits on the trays.

Melting moments

PREP + COOK TIME **40 MINUTES + COOLING** | MAKES **20**

Consistency is the key with biscuits such as these. You need uniform-sized biscuits with even markings on top, sandwiched together with equal amounts of buttercream filling. The result will be wonderful buttery biscuits that melt in the mouth.

250g butter, softened
1 tsp vanilla extract
$^{1}/_{2}$ cup (80g) icing sugar
$1^{1}/_{2}$ cups (225g) plain flour
$^{1}/_{2}$ cup (75g) cornflour
2 tsp icing sugar, extra

buttercream
90g butter, chopped
$^{3}/_{4}$ cup (120g) icing sugar
1 tsp finely grated lemon rind
1 tsp lemon juice

1 Preheat oven to 160°C (140°C fan/325°F/Gas 3). Grease two oven trays; line with baking paper.

2 Beat the butter, vanilla, and sifted icing sugar in a small bowl with an electric mixer until pale and fluffy. Transfer the mixture to a large bowl; stir in the sifted flour and cornflour, in two batches.

3 With floured hands, roll rounded teaspoons of the mixture into balls (you should have 40 balls); place 2.5cm apart on trays. Flatten each ball slightly with a floured fork into 4cm rounds.

4 Bake the biscuits for 15 minutes or until a biscuit can be pushed gently without breaking. Leave the biscuits on trays for 5 minutes before transferring to wire racks to cool.

5 Make the buttercream. Beat the butter, sifted icing sugar, and lemon rind in a small bowl with an electric mixer until pale and fluffy. Beat in the lemon juice until combined.

6 Sandwich the biscuits with buttercream. Just before serving, dust with extra sifted icing sugar.

TIP

Sandwiched biscuits will keep, refrigerated, in an airtight container for up to 3 days. Unfilled, the plain biscuits will keep in an airtight container at room temperature for up to 1 week.

Chocolate caramel slice

PREP + COOK TIME **55 MINUTES + REFRIGERATION** | MAKES **24**

Also known as millionaire's shortbread, this confectionery classic consists of a biscuity base topped with soft caramel fudge and a layer of decadent dark chocolate. For easy slicing, cut into squares with a hot knife.

1 cup (150g) plain flour

½ cup (110g) firmly packed brown sugar

½ cup (40g) desiccated coconut

125g butter, melted

125g butter, extra

2 x 397g cans sweetened condensed milk

¼ cup (90g) golden syrup or treacle

185g dark chocolate, coarsely chopped

2 tsp vegetable oil

1 Preheat oven to 180°C (160°C fan/350°F/Gas 4). Grease a 20cm x 30cm rectangular slice pan; line the bottom and long sides with baking paper, extending the paper 5cm over the sides.

2 Combine the sifted flour, sugar, and coconut in a medium bowl; stir in the melted butter. Press the mixture firmly over the bottom of the slice pan; bake for 15 minutes or until light golden. Remove from oven; cool.

3 Place the extra butter, condensed milk, and golden syrup in a medium saucepan; stir over a low heat until smooth. Pour the mixture over the cooled base. Bake for 20 minutes or until golden brown. Cool.

4 Place the chocolate and vegetable oil in a medium heatproof bowl over a medium saucepan of simmering water (make sure the water doesn't touch the base of the bowl); stir until smooth. Spread the chocolate mixture over the cooled slice. Refrigerate for 30 minutes or until set before cutting with a hot knife.

TIP

This slice will keep in an airtight container for up to 1 week. If the weather is hot, place the container in the fridge.

Honey jumbles

PREP + COOK TIME **35 MINUTES + REFRIGERATION** | MAKES **40**

Sugar and spice come together in these chewy soft-baked honey jumbles, iconic Australian biscuits that date back to the nineteenth century. Gingerbread fingers are topped with pink or white icing to create a biscuit that improves with age.

60g butter

1/2 cup (110g) firmly packed brown sugar

3/4 cup (270g) golden syrup

1 egg, lightly beaten

2 1/2 cups (375g) plain flour

1/2 cup (75g) self-raising flour

1/2 tsp bicarbonate of soda

2 tsp ground ginger

2 tsp mixed spice

icing

1 egg white

1 1/2 cups (240g) icing sugar

1 tbsp lemon juice, approximately

pink food colouring

1 Preheat oven to 160°C (140°C fan/325°F/Gas 3). Grease two large oven trays.

2 Stir the butter, sugar, and golden syrup in a medium saucepan over a low heat until the sugar dissolves. Cool for 10 minutes.

3 Transfer the cooled mixture to a large bowl; stir in the egg and sifted dry ingredients, in two batches. Knead the dough on a floured surface until it loses its stickiness. Wrap in plastic wrap (cling film); refrigerate for 30 minutes.

4 Divide the dough into eight portions. Roll each portion into a 2cm thick sausage; cut each sausage into five 6cm lengths. Place on the oven trays about 3cm apart; round the ends with lightly floured fingers, then flatten the biscuits slightly.

5 Bake the biscuits for 15 minutes or until lightly browned. Cool on trays.

6 Meanwhile, make the icing. Beat the egg white lightly in a small bowl; gradually stir in the sifted icing sugar, then enough lemon juice to make the icing spreadable. Place half the mixture in another small bowl; tint with pink colouring. Cover the bowls containing the two icings with a damp tea towel while in use.

7 Spread the cooled jumbles with the pink and white icing.

TIP

Spray your measuring spoon with a little cooking oil spray before scooping up the golden syrup; this will help prevent the syrup from sticking to the spoon.

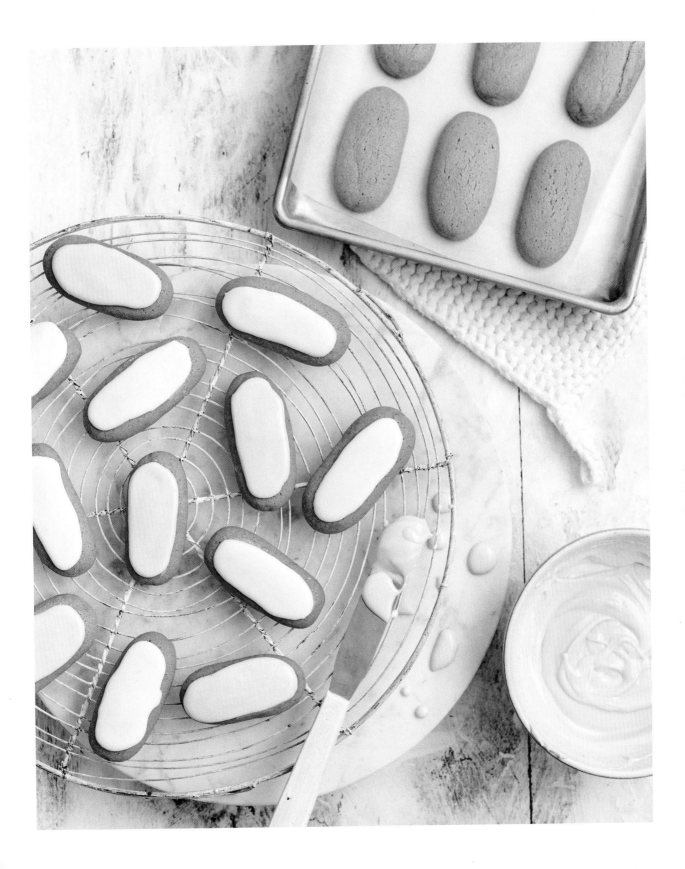

Raspberry coconut slice

PREP + COOK TIME **1 HOUR + COOLING** | MAKES **12**

Here a buttery shortbread base is topped with chunky raspberry jam and toasted flakey coconut for a delectable sweet and fruity slice that's sure to satisfy. This slice is best eaten on the day it's made and is perfect served with morning tea.

90g butter

1/2 cup (110g) caster sugar

1 egg

2/3 cup (100g) plain flour

1/4 cup (35g) self-raising flour

1 tbsp custard powder

1/3 cup (110g) raspberry jam

coconut topping

2 cups (180g) desiccated coconut

1/4 cup (55g) caster sugar

2 eggs, lightly beaten

1 Preheat oven to 180°C (160°C fan/350°F/Gas 4). Grease a 19cm x 29cm rectangular slice pan; line the bottom and two long sides with baking paper, extending the paper 2cm over the sides.

2 Beat the butter, sugar, and egg with an electric mixer until changed to a lighter colour. Stir in the sifted flours and custard powder. Spread the mixture over the bottom of the slice pan.

3 Bake the base for 15 minutes. Cool in the pan for 10 minutes.

4 Meanwhile, to make the coconut topping, combine the ingredients in a medium bowl.

5 Spread the jam on the cooled base, sprinkle with the coconut topping. Bake the slice for a further 25 minutes or until lightly browned. Cool in the pan before cutting.

Tangy lemon slice

PREP + COOK TIME **55 MINUTES** | MAKES **16**

A fresh lemon filling sits on a buttery biscuit base to create these sweet and zesty lemon
squares, perfect for a dessert or serving with a cup of tea. Be sure to let the squares
cool completely before cutting.

125g butter, coarsely chopped

$^1/_4$ cup (40g) icing sugar

$1^1/_4$ cups (185g) plain flour

3 eggs

1 cup (220g) caster sugar

2 tsp finely grated lemon rind

$^1/_2$ cup (125ml) lemon juice

1 tbsp icing sugar, extra

1   Preheat oven to 180°C (160°C fan/350°F/Gas 4). Grease a shallow 23cm
square cake pan; line the bottom and sides with baking paper, extending
the paper 2cm above the edge.

2   Beat the butter and icing sugar in a small bowl with an electric mixer
until smooth. Stir in 1 cup (150g) of the flour. Press the mixture evenly
over the bottom of the cake pan.

3   Bake the base for 15 minutes or until lightly browned.

4   Meanwhile, place the eggs, caster sugar, remaining flour, the lemon rind
and juice in a medium bowl; whisk until combined. Pour the lemon filling
over the hot base.

5   Bake for a further 20 minutes or until firm. Cool in the pan on a wire rack
before cutting into squares. Just before serving, dust with extra sifted
icing sugar.

TIP

This slice will keep, stored in an airtight container
in the fridge, for up to 3 days.

Berry jam and vanilla palmiers

PREP + COOK TIME **30 MINUTES + FREEZING AND COOLING** | MAKES **46**

Palmiers are delicious French pastries that can be served either for breakfast or dessert. In this recipe you can use your favourite flavour of berry jam including strawberry, raspberry, blackberry, or mixed berry.

½ cup (60g) flaked almonds, very finely chopped

1 tsp vanilla bean paste

1 tsp finely grated orange rind

⅔ cup (215g) berry jam (see tip)

2 sheets puff pastry

2 tbsp caster sugar

1 Combine the almonds, vanilla paste, orange rind, and jam in a small bowl.

2 Spread the jam mixture evenly over the pastry sheets. Fold the two opposite sides of the pastry inward to meet in the middle; flatten slightly. Repeat the fold again and flatten slightly. Fold again so the outside edges of the pastry meet. Roll the pastry in sugar, then wrap each roll, separately, in plastic wrap (cling film); freeze for 30 minutes or until slightly firm.

3 Preheat oven to 180°C (160°C fan/350°F/Gas 4). Line two large oven trays with baking paper.

4 Remove then discard the plastic wrap (cling film) from the pastry rolls; cut the pastry into 1cm slices. Place the slices, cut-side up, 5cm apart on the oven trays.

5 Bake the palmiers for 20 minutes or until puffed and golden. Leave to cool on the trays.

TIP

You can also use another flavour jam such as apricot, or even marmalade.

Florentine biscotti

PREP + COOK TIME **1 HOUR 20 MINUTES + COOLING AND STANDING** | MAKES **70**

Biscotti are twice-baked Italian almond biscuits. Because of their dry texture they are often served with a drink, into which they can be dunked – traditionally after dinner with the Tuscan fortified wine, vin santo. These days they are more commonly consumed with coffee.

1 cup (220g) caster sugar

2 eggs

1 cup (150g) plain flour

cup (75g) self-raising flour

³/₄ cup (60g) flaked almonds, roasted

¹/₂ cup (80g) sultanas

¹/₂ cup (100g) red glacé cherries, halved

200g dark chocolate, chopped

1 Preheat oven to 180°C (160°C fan/350°F/Gas 4). Grease and line two large oven trays with baking paper.

2 Whisk the sugar and eggs in a medium bowl until combined; stir in the sifted flours, almonds, sultanas, and glacé cherries. Shape the dough into two 30cm logs. Place on trays; flatten slightly.

3 Bake the logs for about 30 minutes. Cool on the trays.

4 Reduce oven temperature to 140°C (120°C fan/275°F/Gas 1).

5 Using a serrated knife, slice logs diagonally into 5mm slices. Place the slices, in a single layer, on the baking-paper-lined oven trays. Bake for 20 minutes, turning halfway through baking, or until dry and crisp. Cool on wire racks.

6 Place the chocolate in a medium heatproof bowl over a medium saucepan of simmering water (make sure the base of the bowl doesn't touch the water); stir until melted. Transfer the chocolate to a small cup. Dip one end of the biscotti into chocolate; drain off any excess. Place the biscotti on the baking-paper-lined trays. Stand at room temperature until the chocolate sets.

TIP

Biscotti will keep in an airtight container for up to 2 weeks.

Gingerbread wreaths

PREP + COOK TIME **1 HOUR + REFRIGERATION** | MAKES **2 WREATHS** OR **30 MEDIUM-SIZED BISCUITS**

You will need three or four different-sized star cutters to make these wreaths. We used 8cm, 6cm, 5cm, and 3cm. We have included a recipe for royal icing, which you can also use to ice the stars on the wreath if you like, or it can be used to decorate any other shape.

125g butter, softened

½ cup (110g) firmly packed brown sugar

1 egg yolk

2¾ cups (405g) plain flour

1 tsp bicarbonate of soda

3 tsp ground ginger

½ cup (125ml) golden syrup or treacle

icing sugar, to dust

royal icing

1 egg white

1½ cups (240g) icing sugar, approximately

1 Beat the butter and sugar in a small bowl with an electric mixer until combined. Beat in the egg yolk. Stir in the sifted dry ingredients and golden syrup to form a soft dough. Knead the dough on a floured surface until smooth. Divide the dough in half; enclose in plastic wrap (cling film), and refrigerate for 1 hour.

2 Roll each portion of dough between sheets of baking paper until 5mm thick. Freeze for 15 minutes to firm.

3 Preheat oven to 180°C (160°C fan/350°F/Gas 4). Line two oven trays with baking paper.

4 Cut out 24 large, 12 medium, 16 small, and 16 smallest stars with cutters, re-rolling scraps of dough as necessary. Place the two smaller sized stars on one tray and the medium and large stars on the second tray.

5 Bake the larger stars for 15 minutes and the smaller stars for 12 minutes, or until lightly coloured; cool on the trays.

6 Meanwhile, make the royal icing. Beat the egg white in a small bowl with an electric mixer until frothy; gradually beat in enough sifted icing sugar until the mixture is a piping consistency. Keep the icing covered with a damp tea towel to prevent it drying out.

7 Draw a 25cm round on two pieces of baking paper, turn the paper, marked-side down on a work surface. Spoon the icing into a piping bag fitted with a small plain tube (see tips). Following the shape of the marked circle, arrange the stars into a wreath shape "gluing" stars to one another with the icing. Stand the wreaths at room temperature until set. Just before serving, dust with icing sugar.

TIPS

▪ If you don't have a piping bag, you can use a plastic zip lock bag instead.

▪ Biscuits will keep in an airtight container at room temperature for up to 2 weeks.

Slice-and-bake biscuits

PREP + COOK TIME **1 HOUR 30 MINUTES + REFRIGERATION** | MAKES **48**

This super simple recipe results in delicious buttery biscuits that are perfect for lunchboxes, homemade gifts, or to enjoy with a cup of tea. The biscuit dough rolls can be wrapped in foil and frozen for up to 1 month.

250g butter

1¼ cups (200g) icing sugar

2 tsp vanilla extract

2 cups (300g) plain flour

½ cup (75g) rice flour

⅓ cup (50g) cornflour

2 tbsp milk

1 tbsp icing sugar, extra

1 Beat the butter, sugar, and vanilla extract in a large bowl with an electric mixer until pale and fluffy. Stir in the combined sifted flours, in two batches, then the milk until mixed well.

2 Divide the mixture in half. Knead each half on a floured surface until smooth; roll the halves into 25cm logs. Wrap each log in baking paper; refrigerate for 1 hour until firm or for up to 2 days.

3 Preheat oven to 160°C (140°C fan/325°F/Gas 3). Grease two oven trays. Cut the logs into 1cm slices; place the rounds 3cm apart on the oven trays.

4 Bake the biscuits for 20 minutes or until pale golden, turning the trays halfway through baking. Stand the biscuits on the trays for 20 minutes, before transferring to wire racks to cool. Dust with extra icing sugar before serving.

TIP

These biscuits will keep in an airtight container for up to 1 week.

Slice-and-bake biscuit variations

For these colourful nutty, chocolatey, or zingy variations of slice-and-bake biscuits, make the plain version on page 35 omitting, swapping, and adding ingredients as directed in the individual recipes below.

Orange and poppy seed

Make the slice-and-bake biscuits, omitting the vanilla extract and beating in 1 tablespoon finely grated orange rind with the butter and icing sugar; add 1½ tablespoons poppy seeds with the combined sifted flours. Continue as directed in the recipe.

Pecan and cinnamon

Make the slice-and-bake biscuits, adding 1 teaspoon ground cinnamon to the sifted flours and stirring in 1 cup (100g) roasted chopped pecans. Before baking, sprinkle the sliced biscuits with 2 tablespoons cinnamon sugar. Continue as directed in the recipe.

M&M's

Make the slice-and-bake biscuits, adding in 230g M&M's with the combined sifted flours, in batches. Continue as directed in the recipe.

Lemon and pistachios

Make the slice-and-bake biscuits, omitting the vanilla extract and beating in 1 tablespoon finely grated lemon rind with the butter and icing sugar. Stir in ¾ cup (110g) roasted chopped pistachios with the combined sifted flours. Continue as directed in the recipe.

TIP

Colour from the M&M's may bleed a little into the dough.

Chocolate truffle almond slice

PREP + COOK TIME **1 HOUR 10 MINUTES + REFRIGERATION** | MAKES **24**

Almonds and dark chocolate are combined to create these decadent mouthwatering truffle triangles that are perfect for an after-dinner treat. Alternatively, present them in a beautiful ribboned box and gift them to someone special.

150g dark chocolate, coarsely chopped

3 egg whites

3/4 cup (165g) caster sugar

1 cup (120g) almond meal

2 tbsp plain flour

1 tbsp cocoa powder

topping

200g dark chocolate, coarsely chopped

125g butter, chopped

1/3 cup (75g) caster sugar

3 egg yolks

1 Preheat oven to 180°C (160°C fan/350°F/Gas 4). Grease a 20cm x 30cm rectangular slice pan; line the bottom and two long sides with baking paper, extending the paper 5cm over the sides.

2 Place the chocolate in a small heatproof bowl over a small saucepan of simmering water (make sure the base of the bowl doesn't touch the water); stir until melted. Spread the chocolate over the base of the slice pan. Refrigerate for 10 minutes or until set.

3 Beat the egg whites in a small bowl with an electric mixer until soft peaks form; gradually add the sugar, beating until dissolved between additions. Fold in the almond meal and flour. Spread the mixture over the chocolate base.

4 Bake for 20 minutes or until firm; cool for 5 minutes.

5 To make the topping, place the chocolate in a small heatproof bowl over a small saucepan of simmering water (make sure the base of the bowl doesn't touch the water); stir until melted. Beat the butter, sugar, and egg yolks in a small bowl with an electric mixer until the sugar dissolves. Add the melted chocolate; stir until smooth.

6 Spread the topping over the slice. Bake for a further 15 minutes or until set; cool. Refrigerate until firm. Before serving, dust with cocoa; cut into triangles.

Peanut butter cookies

PREP + COOK TIME **50 MINUTES + REFRIGERATION** | MAKES **24**

The robust peanut taste and crisp chewy texture of these cookies will ensure they are a firm favourite with the whole family. The perfect balance of salty and sweet, and a melt-in-your-mouth texture makes them an instant cookie classic.

60g butter, softened

$1/2$ cup (130g) smooth peanut butter

$1/2$ cup (110g) caster sugar

$1/2$ cup (110g) firmly packed brown sugar

1 egg

1 cup (140g) roasted unsalted peanuts, coarsely chopped

40g chocolate-coated honeycomb bar, coarsely chopped

1 cup (150g) self-raising flour

1 Preheat oven to 180°C (160°C fan/350°F/Gas 4). Grease three large oven trays; line each with baking paper.

2 Beat the butter, peanut butter, and sugars in a small bowl with an electric mixer until pale and fluffy. Beat in the egg until just combined. Stir in the peanuts and honeycomb, then the sifted flour.

3 Roll $1/2$ tablespoons of mixture into balls; place 3cm apart on the oven trays. Flatten the mixture slightly, pushing any nuts or honeycomb back into the mixture if they fall out.

4 Bake the cookies for 15 minutes or until lightly browned. Cool on the trays.

Anzac biscuits

PREP + COOK TIME **45 MINUTES** | MAKES **32**

Anzac biscuits were baked by volunteers and packed in billycans to be sent to soldiers during WWI. Now these oaty golden biscuits are traditionally eaten in Australia and New Zealand for Anzac Day, a day of remembrance to commemorate servicemen and women, past and present.

125g butter, chopped

2 tbsp golden syrup or treacle

½ teaspoon bicarbonate of soda

2 tbsp boiling water

1 cup (90g) rolled oats (see tip)

1 cup (150g) plain flour

1 cup (220g) firmly packed brown sugar

¾ cup (60g) desiccated coconut

1   Preheat oven to 180°C/350°F. Grease two large oven trays; line with baking paper.

2   Stir the butter and syrup in a medium saucepan over a low heat until smooth. Stir in the combined bicarbonate of soda and water, then the remaining ingredients.

3   Roll level tablespoons of mixture into balls; place 5cm apart on lined trays, then flatten slightly.

4   Bake the biscuits for 15 minutes or until golden. Cool the biscuits on the trays.

TIP

Make sure you use rolled oats rather than quick-cooking oats as they will produce a different result.

CAKES AND CUPCAKES

Everything from classic cakes to decadent
dessert cakes and celebratory centrepieces
can be found in this delightful collection
of sweet bakes.

One-bowl chocolate velvet cake

PREP + COOK TIME **1 HOUR 10 MINUTES + REFRIGERATION** | SERVES **16**

This simple and quick one-bowl recipe results in a moist decadent cake topped with an indulgent chocolate glaze that's certain to be a crowd pleaser. Make sure your cake has cooled completely before spreading the glaze.

125g butter, softened

1 cup (220g) firmly packed brown sugar

1/2 cup (110g) caster sugar

3 eggs

2 cups (300g) plain flour

1/3 cup (35g) cocoa powder

1 tsp bicarbonate of soda

2/3 cup (160g) sour cream

1/2 cup (125ml) water

chocolate glaze

90g dark chocolate, coarsely chopped

60g butter, coarsely chopped

1/2 cup (80g) icing sugar

1/4 cup (60g) sour cream

1 Preheat oven to 180°C (160°C fan/350°F/Gas 4). Grease a deep 23cm x 30cm rectangular cake pan or baking dish; line the bottom and two long sides with baking paper, extending the paper 5cm over the sides.

2 Beat the cake ingredients in a large bowl with an electric mixer on low speed until just combined. Increase the speed to medium; beat for about 3 minutes or until the mixture is smooth and paler in colour. Spread the mixture into the cake pan.

3 Bake the cake for 45 minutes or until a skewer inserted into the centre comes out clean. Leave in the pan for 10 minutes before turning, top-side up, onto a wire rack to cool.

4 Meanwhile, make the chocolate glaze. Stir the ingredients in a small saucepan over a low heat until smooth; cook, stirring, for 2 minutes. Transfer the mixture to a small bowl; cool for 10 minutes. Refrigerate for 20 minutes or until the glaze is spreadable.

5 Spread the chocolate glaze over the top of the cold cake; stand until set before cutting.

TIPS

- This cake will keep in an airtight container, at room temperature, for up to 3 days.
- Without the glaze, the cake can be frozen for up to 2 months.

New York cheesecake

PREP + COOK TIME **2 HOURS 30 MINUTES + REFRIGERATION** | SERVES **12**

New York-style cheesecake is twice-baked and thanks to lashings of cream cheese has a rich, dense, smooth, and creamy texture. To slice the cheesecake, first dip the knife in hot water so it easily glides through the filling to produce a neat slice.

500g plain sweet biscuits
250g butter, melted
750g cream cheese, softened
2 tsp finely grated orange rind
1 tsp finely grated lemon rind
1 cup (220g) caster sugar
3 eggs
$^3/_4$ cup (180g) sour cream
$^1/_4$ cup (60ml) lemon juice

sour cream topping
1 cup (240g) sour cream
2 tbsp caster sugar
2 tsp lemon juice

1 Process the biscuits until fine crumbs form; transfer to a large bowl. Add the butter; stir through the crumbs until evenly combined. Press the biscuit mixture over the bottom and side of a 24cm springform pan. Place the pan on an oven tray; refrigerate for 30 minutes.

2 Preheat oven to 180°C (160°C fan/350°F/Gas 4).

3 Beat the cream cheese, orange rind, lemon rind, and sugar in a medium bowl with an electric mixer until smooth. Beat in the eggs, one at a time, then the sour cream and lemon juice. Pour the filling into the pan.

4 Bake the cheesecake for $1^1/_4$ hours; remove from the oven. Cool for 15 minutes.

5 Meanwhile, make the sour cream topping. Stir the ingredients together in a medium bowl with a wooden spoon until smooth. (Don't use a whisk as you don't want to create bubbles in the mixture.)

6 Spread the sour cream topping over the cheesecake. Bake for a further 20 minutes. Turn the oven off; cool the cheesecake in the oven with the door ajar. Refrigerate the cold cheesecake for 3 hours or overnight, before serving.

TIPS

- Make sure all ingredients are at room temperature before you start this recipe.
- Store the cheesecake in an airtight container in the fridge.

Blackberry swirl lemonade cupcakes

PREP + COOK TIME **1 HOUR + FREEZING** | MAKES **12**

These sweet and satisfying cupcakes are perfect for morning or afternoon tea. Use a clear, carbonated lemonade for this recipe. If you have any leftover frosting, keep it in the freezer for another batch of cupcakes.

125g butter, softened

$1/2$ cup (110g) caster sugar

1 tbsp finely grated lemon rind

2 eggs

$1^1/2$ cups (225g) self-raising flour

$1/2$ cup (125ml) lemonade

blackberry swirl frosting

$1/4$ cup (35g) frozen blackberries, thawed

500g cream cheese, softened

2 cups (320g) icing sugar

1 tbsp lemonade

2 tsp finely grated lemon rind

1 Make the blackberry swirl frosting. Crush the blackberries well with a fork. Beat the cream cheese, sifted icing sugar, lemonade, and lemon rind in a small bowl with an electric mixer until smooth. Lightly fold the crushed berries through the cream cheese mixture to create a swirled effect (don't over-mix or you will lose the swirl); transfer to a freezer-proof container. Cover with plastic wrap (cling film). Freeze for 6 hours or overnight until firm.

2 Preheat oven to 180°C (160°C fan/350°F/Gas 4). Line a 12-hole ($1/3$ cup/ 80ml) muffin pan with paper cases.

3 Beat the butter, sugar, and lemon rind in a small bowl with an electric mixer until light and fluffy. Beat in the eggs, one at a time. Transfer the mixture to a large bowl; stir in the sifted flour and lemonade, in two batches. Spoon the mixture evenly into the paper cases.

4 Bake the cupcakes for 20 minutes or until a skewer inserted into the centre comes out clean. Leave the cakes in the pan for 5 minutes before turning, top-side up, onto a wire rack to cool.

5 Just before serving, use a small ice-cream scoop to place the frosting on top of the cupcakes.

Coffee and walnut cake

PREP + COOK TIME **1 HOUR 15 MINUTES + COOLING AND STANDING** | SERVES **8**

This classic combo is nostalgic sweet comfort food at its best. Topping the cake with
a drizzle of toffee adds another layer of scrumptious, decadent indulgence, perfect for
an afternoon tea treat.

30g butter

1 tbsp brown sugar

2 tsp ground cinnamon

2 cups (200g) roasted walnuts

1/2 cup (125ml) milk

1 tbsp instant coffee granules

185g butter, softened, extra

1 1/3 cups (300g) caster sugar

3 eggs

1 cup (150g) self-raising flour

3/4 cup (110g) plain flour

toffee drizzle

1/2 cup (110g) caster sugar

1/4 cup (60ml) water

1/4 cup (60ml) single cream

1 Preheat oven to 160°C (140°C fan/325°F/Gas 3). Grease a 22cm baba cake pan well; dust with flour, shake out the excess.

2 Melt the butter in a small saucepan over a medium heat; stir in the brown sugar, cinnamon, and walnuts. Cool.

3 Combine the milk and coffee in a small bowl; stir well until the coffee dissolves.

4 Beat the extra butter and caster sugar in a small bowl with an electric mixer until light and fluffy. Beat in the eggs, one at a time. Stir in the sifted flours, then the milk mixture. Spread one-third of the cake mixture over the bottom of the pan; sprinkle with one-third of the walnut mixture. Top with the remaining cake mixture.

5 Bake the cake for 55 minutes. Leave in the pan for 5 minutes before turning onto a wire rack over an oven tray. Cool.

6 Make the toffee drizzle. Stir the sugar and water in a small saucepan over a medium heat, without boiling, until the sugar dissolves; bring to the boil. Reduce heat; simmer, without stirring, until caramel in colour. Add the cream; stir for 1 minute or until the mixture has thickened slightly.

7 Working quickly, drizzle the toffee on top of the cake; top with the remaining walnut mixture, pressing down lightly.

Almond friands

PREP + COOK TIME **45 MINUTES** | MAKES **12**

Friands, known in France as financiers, are delightful little almond-based cakes. They are
great for parties, picnics, or a lunchbox treat. Alternatively, serve after dinner as a petit four.
See pages 56–57 for delicious variations.

6 egg whites

185g butter, melted

1 cup (120g) almond meal

1½ cups (240g) icing sugar

½ cup (75g) plain flour

1 tbsp icing sugar, extra

1 Preheat oven to 200°C (180°C fan/400°F/Gas 6).

2 Grease a 12-hole (½-cup/125ml) oval friand pan or rectangular mini loaf
pan tray.

3 Place the egg whites in a medium bowl, stir with a fork. Add the
remaining ingredients to the bowl; stir until just combined. Spoon the
mixture into the pan holes.

4 Bake for 20 minutes. Leave the friands in the pan for 5 minutes before
transferring to a wire rack to cool. Serve dusted with a little extra sifted
icing sugar.

Almond friand variations

Almond friands can easily be adapted to accommodate your favourite flavour combinations. Make the plain version on page 55 omitting, swapping, and adding ingredients as directed in the individual recipes below.

Raspberry and white chocolate

TOP LEFT Stir 100g coarsely chopped white chocolate into the friand mixture. Spoon into the holes; top with 100g fresh or frozen raspberries.

Chocolate and hazelnut

MIDDLE LEFT Use hazelnut meal instead of almond. Stir 100g chopped dark chocolate into the friand mixture. Spoon into the holes; top with 1/4 cup (35g) chopped hazelnuts.

Plum

BOTTOM LEFT Use hazelnut or almond meal in the friand mixture. Spoon into the holes; top with 2 medium (200g) thinly sliced plums. Bake as directed in the recipe.

Passionfruit and lemon syrup cake

TOP RIGHT Use either hazelnut or almond meal in the friand mixture. Spoon into the holes; top with the pulp of 2 medium passionfruit.

Lime and coconut

MIDDLE RIGHT Stir 2 teaspoons of grated lime rind, 1 tablespoon of lime juice, and 1/4 cup (20g) desiccated coconut into the friand mixture. Spoon into the holes; top with flaked coconut.

Lemon curd

BOTTOM RIGHT Stir 2 teaspoons of finely grated lemon rind into the friand mixture. Brush the baked friands with 1/4 cup (80g) store-bought or homemade lemon curd. Cool. Serve topped with extra curd.

Apple ginger cakes with lemon icing

PREP + COOK TIME **35 MINUTES** | MAKES **12**

The warm comforting flavours of apple and ginger are combined to make these mouthwatering little cakes with an autumnal twist. Dripping in lemon icing that brings a sweet zingy dimension, they are sure to be a hit with your guests.

250g butter, softened

1½ cups (330g) firmly packed dark brown sugar

3 eggs

¼ cup (90g) golden syrup

2 cups (300g) plain flour

1½ tsp bicarbonate of soda

2 tbsp ground ginger

1 tbsp ground cinnamon

1 cup (170g) coarsely grated apple (see tips)

⅔ cup (160ml) hot water

lemon icing

2 cups (320g) icing sugar

2 tsp butter, softened

⅓ cup (80ml) lemon juice

1 Preheat oven to 180°C (160°C fan/350°F/Gas 4). Grease two 6-hole (¾ cup/ 180ml) mini bundt pans or two 6-hole (¾ cup/180ml) texas muffin pans.

2 Beat the butter and sugar in a small bowl with an electric mixer until paler and fluffy. Beat in the eggs, one at a time, until well combined between additions. Stir in the golden syrup.

3 Transfer the mixture to a medium bowl; stir in the sifted dry ingredients, then the apple and the water.

4 Divide the mixture among the pan holes, smooth the surface.

5 Bake the cakes for 25 minutes or until a skewer inserted into the centre comes out clean. Leave the cakes in the pans for 5 minutes before turning onto wire racks to cool.

6 Make the lemon icing. Sift the icing sugar into a medium heatproof bowl; stir in the butter and lemon juice to form a paste. Place the bowl over a small saucepan of simmering water; stir until the icing is of a pouring consistency.

7 Before serving, drizzle the lemon icing over the cakes.

TIPS

- You will need 1 large apple (200g) for this recipe.
- Cakes will keep in an airtight container for up to 3 days.
- Un-iced cakes can be frozen for up to 3 months.

Featherlight sponge

PREP + COOK TIME **40 MINUTES + STANDING** | SERVES **10**

This recipe results in the lightest, fluffiest cake perfect for afternoon tea or picnics in the sunshine. This classic version includes a cream filling but you could also add a layer of strawberry jam and top with sliced strawberries.

4 eggs

3/4 cup (165g) caster sugar

1 cup (150g) wheaten cornflour

1/4 cup (30g) custard powder

1 tsp cream of tartar

1/2 tsp bicarbonate of soda

300ml thickened (whipping) cream

1 tbsp icing sugar

1 Preheat oven to 200°C (180°C fan/400°F/Gas 6). Grease and flour two deep 20cm round cake pans; shake out the excess flour.

2 Beat the eggs and caster sugar in a large bowl with an electric mixer for 7 minutes until thick and creamy. To test if the mixture is ready, turn off the mixer then lift the beaters; the mixture should form thick ribbons. (If you are using hand-held electric beaters, use a small bowl for beating the eggs and sugar, then transfer to a large bowl to stir in the dry ingredients.)

3 Sift the dry ingredients twice onto a piece of baking paper. Sift the flour mixture a third time evenly onto the egg mixture. Using a balloon whisk or large metal spoon, quickly and lightly fold the flour mixture through the egg mixture until combined.

4 Divide the mixture evenly between the pans; tilt the pans to spread the mixture to the edge. (To ensure the quantity in each pan is exactly the same, place a cake pan on a set of scales, set the display to zero; fill each pan, adjusting the mixture until both pans weigh the same.)

5 Bake the sponges for 20 minutes or until they spring back when pressed lightly in the centre. Turn the sponges immediately, top-side up, onto baking-paper-covered wire racks. Cool.

6 Beat the cream in a large bowl until soft peaks form.

7 Serve the sponge filled with the cream and dusted with icing sugar.

Classic butter cake

PREP + COOK TIME **1 HOUR 30 MINUTES** | SERVES **12**

This moist butter cake is so simple to make, requiring just a handful of ingredients, and is perfect to serve for morning or afternoon tea. It also makes a great a celebration cake – add frostings or toppings as you wish. Best made on the day of serving.

250g butter, softened

2 tsp vanilla bean paste

1½ cups (330g) caster sugar

3 eggs

1¾ cups (260g) self-raising flour

⅓ cup (50g) plain flour

¾ cup (180ml) milk

vanilla bean icing

1½ cups (240g) icing sugar

1 tsp vanilla bean paste

2 tbsp water, approximately

1 Preheat oven to 160°C (140°C fan/325°F/Gas 3). Grease a deep 20cm square cake pan or deep 22cm round cake pan, line the bottom and sides of the pan with baking paper, extending the paper 5cm above the sides.

2 Beat the butter, vanilla paste, and sugar in a medium bowl with an electric mixer until light and fluffy. Add the eggs one at a time, beating until just combined between additions. Transfer the mixture to a large bowl; fold in the combined sifted flours and milk in two batches. Spread the mixture into the pan.

3 Bake the cake for 1 hour 10 minutes or until a skewer inserted into the centre comes out clean. Leave the cake in the pan for 5 minutes before turning onto a wire rack to cool.

4 Make the vanilla bean icing. Sift the icing sugar into a small heatproof bowl; stir in the vanilla and enough water to form a firm paste. Place the bowl over a small saucepan of simmering water; stir until the icing is a spreadable consistency. Do not over-heat.

5 Spread the icing immediately on the cake, allowing a little to drip over the sides.

Marshmallow pavlova

PREP + COOK TIME **2 HOURS 20 MINUTES + COOLING** | SERVES **10**

With its soft, fluffy, marshmallowy centre and sweet crunchy exterior topped with lashings of cream and fruit this pavlova is sure to wow your guests. It can be baked a day ahead; store in an airtight container in a cool dry place. Assemble with cream and fruit close to serving.

6 egg whites

pinch of cream of tartar

1^1/$_2$ cups (330g) caster sugar

3 tsp cornflour

2 tsp vanilla bean paste

1^1/$_2$ tsp white vinegar

1^3/$_4$ cups (430ml) thickened (whipping) cream

250g blueberries

125g raspberries

1 tbsp icing sugar

1 Preheat oven to 120°C (100 °C fan /250°F/Gas^1/$_2$). Grease an oven tray. Mark a 20cm circle on a sheet of baking paper; place the paper, marked-side down, on the tray.

2 Whisk the egg whites and cream of tartar in a medium bowl with an electric mixer until soft peaks form. Gradually add the sugar, beating until the sugar has dissolved after each addition and the mixture is thick and glossy. Fold in the sifted cornflour, then the vanilla paste and vinegar. Spread the meringue inside the marked round on the tray; build up the side to about 10cm high and flatten the top.

3 Bake the pavlova for 1 hour 45 minutes or until dry to touch. Turn the oven off; cool pavlova in the oven with the door ajar.

4 Just before serving, beat the cream in a small bowl with an electric mixer until soft peaks form. Spoon the cream on the pavlova, top with blueberries and raspberries. Dust with icing sugar.

Chocolate slab cake

PREP + COOK TIME **1 HOUR 20 MINUTES** | SERVES **20**

Choose a perfectly level-bottomed roasting pan to bake this deliciously moist chocolate cake. If the cake appears to be cooking too quickly, reduce the oven temperature to 160°C (140°C fan/325°F/Gas 3); this will increase the cooking time by up to 15 minutes.

3 cups (660g) caster sugar

250g butter, chopped

2 cups (500ml) water

1/3 cup (35g) cocoa powder

1 tsp bicarbonate of soda

3 cups (450g) self-raising flour

4 eggs, beaten lightly

chocolate buttercream

125g butter

1 1/2 cups (240g) icing sugar

1/3 cup (35g) cocoa powder

2 tbsp milk

1 Preheat oven to 180°C (160°C fan/350°F/Gas 4). Grease a deep 26.5cm x 33cm, 14 cup (3.5 litre) roasting pan; line the bottom with baking paper.

2 Place the sugar, butter, water, and combined sifted cocoa and bicarbonate of soda in a large saucepan; stir over a medium-low heat, without boiling, until the sugar dissolves and the butter has melted. Bring to the boil. Reduce the heat to low; simmer, for 5 minutes. Transfer the mixture to a large bowl; cool to room temperature.

3 Add the flour and egg to the chocolate mixture; beat with an electric mixer until the mixture is smooth and paler in colour. Pour the mixture into the pan.

4 Bake the cake for 50 minutes or until a skewer inserted into the centre comes out clean. Leave the cake in the pan for 5 minutes before turning out, top-side up, on a wire rack to cool.

5 Make the chocolate buttercream. Beat the butter in a small bowl with an electric mixer until as white as possible. Gradually beat in half the sifted icing sugar and cocoa powder, then the milk and remaining icing sugar and cocoa powder.

6 Spread the cold cake with the buttercream. Decorate with chocolate shavings, if you like.

TIPS

- This cake will keep for up to 2 days in an airtight container at room temperature, or in the refrigerator for up to 4 days.
- Frosted or unfrosted, the cake can be frozen for up to 3 months.

Carrot cake

PREP + COOK TIME **1 HOUR 30 MINUTES** | SERVES **12**

This classic cake is easy to make and really versatile, simply delicious as it is served
with a hot cup of tea or coffee – or add one of the mouthwatering frostings on pages 70–71
to bring in some of your favourite flavours.

3 eggs

1¹/₃ cups (295g) firmly packed brown sugar

1 cup (250ml) vegetable oil

3 cups coarsely grated carrot

1 cup (120g) coarsely chopped walnuts

2¹/₂ cups (375g) self-raising flour

¹/₂ tsp bicarbonate of soda

2 tsp mixed spice

1   Preheat oven to 180°C (160°C fan/350°F/Gas 4). Grease a deep 22cm round
    cake pan; line the bottom with baking paper.

2   Beat the eggs, sugar, and oil in a small bowl with an electric mixer until
    thick and creamy. Transfer the mixture to a large bowl; stir in the carrot
    and walnuts, then the sifted dry ingredients. Pour the mixture into
    the pan.

3   Bake the cake for 1 hour 15 minutes. Leave in the pan for 5 minutes before
    turning, top-side up, onto a wire rack to cool. Serve the cake dusted with
    a little icing sugar, if you like.

Carrot cake variations

Try topping your carrot cake with one of these delicious frostings – delectably creamy and sweet they'll take your bake to another level. Make the plain version on page 69, split your cake to add your chosen frosting, and lastly spread it on top of the cooled cake.

Lemon cream cheese frosting

Beat 100g softened butter, 250g softened cream cheese, and 2 teaspoons of finely grated lemon rind in a small bowl with an electric mixer until light and fluffy. Gradually beat in $3^{1}/_{3}$ cups (540g) icing sugar until combined. Split the carrot cake in half; spread the bottom layer with half the frosting. Top with the remaining cake and the frosting.

Ricotta ginger frosting

Process $1^{1}/_{2}$ cups (360g) firm ricotta with 2 tablespoons of honey until smooth. Transfer the ricotta mixture to a small bowl; fold through $^{1}/_{4}$ cup (55g) finely chopped crystallised ginger. Refrigerate the frosting for 1 hour or until the mixture becomes firmer. Split the carrot cake in half; spread the bottom layer with half the frosting. Top with the remaining cake and the frosting.

Marmalade cream cheese frosting

Beat 100g softened butter and 250g softened cream cheese in a small bowl with an electric mixer until light and fluffy. Gradually beat in $^{3}/_{4}$ cup (255g) orange marmalade, followed by 2 cups (320g) icing sugar until combined. Split the carrot cake in half; spread the bottom layer with half the frosting. Top with the remaining cake and the frosting.

Maple cream cheese frosting

Beat 100g softened butter, 250g softened cream cheese, and 1 teaspoon of vanilla extract with an electric mixer until fluffy. Gradually beat in $3^{1}/_{3}$ cups sifted icing sugar, then $^{1}/_{4}$ cup (60ml) pure maple syrup. Refrigerate for 30 minutes to firm. Split the carrot cake in half; spread the bottom layer with half the frosting. Top with the remaining cake and the frosting.

Caramel éclairs

PREP + COOK TIME **1 HOUR 15 MINUTES + COOLING** | MAKES **12**

Filled with caramel cream and topped with coffee icing, these rich and delicious French pastries will become an instant favourite. Unfilled pastry cases can be made a day ahead but the éclairs are best filled, iced, and assembled close to serving.

1 cup (250ml) water

75g unsalted butter, finely chopped

1 tbsp dark brown sugar

1 cup (150g) bread flour

4 eggs

³/₄ cup (180ml) thickened (whipping) cream

1 cup (300g) dulce de leche (see tip)

coffee icing

1 cup (160g) icing sugar

1¹/₂ tbsp freshly made espresso coffee

1 Preheat oven to 220°C (200°C fan/425°F/Gas 7). Grease two oven trays.

2 To make the choux pastry, place the water, butter, and sugar in a medium saucepan; bring to the boil. Add the flour; beat with a wooden spoon over a medium heat until the mixture comes away from the bottom and side of the pan. Transfer the pastry to a medium bowl of an electric mixer. Beat in the eggs, one at a time, until the mixture is smooth and glossy.

3 Spoon the pastry into a piping bag fitted with 1.5cm plain tube. Pipe 12cm lengths on trays, about 5cm apart. Using a finger dipped in water, smooth any rough edges.

4 Bake the éclairs for 10 minutes. Reduce oven to 180°C (160°C fan/350°F/Gas 4); bake for a further 15 minutes. Using a serrated knife, cut the éclair cases in half horizontally; remove any soft doughy centres. Return the cases to the oven trays; bake for a further 5 minutes or until the cases are dry. Cool on the trays.

5 Meanwhile, make the coffee icing. Sift the icing sugar into a medium heatproof bowl. Stir in enough hot coffee to form a thick spreadable icing. Spread the éclair tops with the icing while still warm.

6 Beat the cream in a medium bowl with an electric mixer until almost firm peaks form; gently fold in the dulce de leche. Spoon the cream mixture into a piping bag; pipe into the éclair bases. Position the iced tops on the bases.

TIP

Dulce de leche is sold in jars from supermarkets, gourmet food stores, and delicatessens.

Sticky date pudding with caramel sauce

PREP + COOK TIME **1 HOUR 15 MINUTES** | SERVES **8**

This rich, comforting pudding is the perfect winter warmer. Best eaten hot from the oven with lashings of irresistible caramel sauce. Serve with a scoop of vanilla ice cream or a swirl of whipped cream, if you like.

1½ cups (250g) pitted dried dates
1¼ cups (310ml) boiling water
1 tsp bicarbonate of soda
¾ cup (165g) firmly packed brown sugar
60g butter, chopped
2 eggs
1 cup (150g) self-raising flour

caramel sauce
1 cup (220g) firmly packed brown sugar
300ml pure (single) cream
100g butter, chopped

1 Preheat oven 180°C (160°C fan/350°F/Gas 4). Grease a 22cm round cake pan; line the bottom with baking paper.

2 Place the dates, water, and bicarbonate of soda in the bowl of a food processor; place the lid on the processor, stand for 5 minutes.

3 Add the sugar and butter to the date mixture; pulse the mixture for 5 seconds or until the dates are coarsely chopped. Add the eggs, then the flour; pulse the mixture for 10 seconds or until all the ingredients are combined. Scrape any unmixed flour back into the mixture with a rubber spatula; pulse again to combine the ingredients. Pour the mixture into the cake pan.

4 Bake the pudding for 55 minutes or until a skewer inserted into the centre comes out clean. Leave the pudding in the pan for 5 minutes before turning, top-side up, onto a plate.

5 Make the caramel sauce. Stir the sugar and cream in a medium saucepan over a high heat until the sugar dissolves. Reduce heat to medium; simmer for 5 minutes or until the mixture is reduced slightly. Whisk in the butter, piece by piece, until melted. Remove from the heat.

6 Serve the hot pudding with the warm caramel sauce.

Peanut heaven cupcakes

PREP + COOK TIME **45 MINUTES + REFRIGERATION** | MAKES **12**

Covered in delectable swirls of chocolate and peanut butter frosting and topped with peanut brittle, these deliciously moist nutty chocolate cupcakes are perfect for a teatime treat. Be sure to let the cakes cool completely before adding the frosting.

60g dark chocolate, coarsely chopped

²/₃ cup (160ml) water

90g butter, softened

1 cup (220g) firmly packed brown sugar

2 eggs

²/₃ cup (100g) self-raising flour

2 tbsp cocoa powder

¹/₃ cup (40g) almond meal

250g peanut brittle, coarsely chopped

whipped milk choc peanut frosting

1 cup (250ml) pure (single) cream

400g milk chocolate, coarsely chopped

1 cup (280g) smooth peanut butter

1 Preheat oven to 180°C (160°C fan/350°F/Gas 4). Line a 12-hole (¹/₃ cup/80ml) muffin pan with paper cases.

2 Stir the chocolate and water together in a small saucepan over a low heat until smooth.

3 Beat the butter, sugar, and eggs in a small bowl with an electric mixer until pale and fluffy. Stir in the sifted flour and cocoa, almond meal, and warm chocolate mixture. Spoon the mixture into paper cases.

4 Bake the cupcakes for 20 minutes or until a skewer inserted into the centre comes out with moist crumbs attached. Leave the cakes in the pan for 5 minutes before turning, top-side up, onto a wire rack to cool.

5 Make the whipped milk choc peanut frosting. Bring the cream almost to the boil in a small saucepan; remove from the heat. When the bubbles subside, add the chocolate; stir until smooth. Transfer the mixture to a small bowl. Cover; refrigerate for 30 minutes. Beat the frosting with an electric mixer until light and fluffy.

6 Spoon the frosting into a large piping bag fitted with a plain 1.5cm tube, alternating with spoonfuls of peanut butter to create a marble effect (see tip).

7 Pipe generous swirls of frosting onto the cold cakes; top with the peanut brittle.

TIP

If you don't have a piping bag, spoon the frosting onto the cakes followed by a spoonful of peanut butter; using the back of the spoon, swirl together in an upward direction.

Devil's food cake

PREP + COOK TIME **1 HOUR 15 MINUTES + COOLING** | SERVES **8**

Richer, darker, and fluffier than regular chocolate cake, devil's food cake was a favourite dessert in the early 1900s, so named for its dark, intense, reddish colour. Finished with an indulgent chocolate frosting this is a must bake for any chocolate lover.

180g butter, chopped

1³/₄ cups (385g) caster sugar

3 eggs

1¹/₂ cups (225g) self-raising flour

¹/₂ cup (75g) plain flour

¹/₂ tsp bicarbonate of soda

²/₃ cup (70g) cocoa powder

3 tsp instant espresso coffee

¹/₂ tsp red food colouring

1 cup (250ml) buttermilk

500g mascarpone

1 tbsp icing sugar

1 tbsp cocoa powder, extra

rich chocolate frosting

100g dark chocolate, chopped

100g unsalted butter, chopped

1 Preheat oven to 180°C (160°C fan/350°F/Gas 4). Grease two deep 20cm round cake pans; line the bottoms with baking paper.

2 Beat the butter and sugar in a small bowl with an electric mixer until light and fluffy. Beat in the eggs one at a time. Transfer the mixture to a large bowl; fold in the sifted flours, bicarbonate of soda, and cocoa powder with the combined coffee, food colouring, and buttermilk, in two batches. Divide the mixture into the pans; smooth the surface.

3 Bake the cakes for 45 minutes or until a skewer inserted into the centre comes out clean. Turn the cakes, top-side up, onto wire racks to cool.

4 Meanwhile, make the rich chocolate frosting. Place the chocolate and butter in a small heatproof bowl over a small saucepan of simmering water (make sure the base of the bowl doesn't touch the water); stir until smooth. Remove from the heat. Cool at room temperature until a spreadable consistency, stirring occasionally while cooling.

5 Stir the mascarpone and sifted icing sugar together in a medium bowl until combined.

6 Place one cake on a plate or cake stand; spread with the mascarpone mixture. Top with the second cake; spread with the rich chocolate frosting. Dust with the extra cocoa powder.

TIP

The cakes can be made up to 2 days ahead; store in airtight containers at room temperature. Assemble and decorate on the day of serving.

Lamingtons

PREP + COOK TIME **50 MINUTES** | MAKES **16**

Lamingtons are classic Australian cakes consisting of a moist butter sponge dipped in chocolate and coated in coconut. They're so popular in their native country that July 21st has been designated National Lamington Day.

6 eggs

²/₃ cup (150g) caster sugar

¹/₂ cup (75g) plain flour

¹/₃ cup (50g) self-raising flour

¹/₃ cup (50g) cornflour

2 cups (160g) desiccated coconut

chocolate icing

4 cups (640g) icing sugar

¹/₂ cup (50g) cocoa powder

15g butter, melted

1 cup (250ml) milk

1   Preheat oven to 180°C (160°C fan/350°F/Gas 4). Grease a 20cm x 30cm rectangular slice pan; line the bottom and long sides with baking paper, extending the paper 5cm over the sides.

2   Beat the eggs in a large bowl with an electric mixer for 10 minutes or until thick and creamy. Gradually add the sugar, beating until dissolved between additions. Sift the flours twice onto a piece of baking paper. Sift the flour mixture a third time evenly onto the egg mixture; fold the flour mixture through the egg mixture. Spread the mixture into the pan.

3   Bake the cake for 35 minutes. Turn the cake immediately onto a baking-paper-covered wire rack to cool.

4   Meanwhile, make the chocolate icing. Sift the icing sugar and cocoa into a medium heatproof bowl; stir in the butter and milk. Place the bowl over a medium saucepan of simmering water; stir until the icing is of a coating consistency.

5   Cut the cake into 16 rectangles. Place the coconut in a medium bowl. Dip each piece of cake in the icing; drain off excess. Toss in the coconut. Place the lamingtons on a wire rack to set.

Raspberry and passionfruit mile-high layer cake

PREP + COOK TIME **2 HOURS 15 MINUTES + COOLING** | SERVES **12**

This mile-high cake makes a great centrepiece for any celebratory occasion. Layers of rich buttery sponge cake, passionfruit cream, and raspberries are coated in a meringue frosting to make a picture-perfect statement cake designed to impress.

375g butter, softened

3 cups (660g) caster sugar

1¹/₂ tsp vanilla extract

6 eggs

3 cups (450g) plain flour

¹/₃ cup (50g) self-raising flour

1 cup (250ml) milk

600g raspberries

passionfruit cream

600ml thickened (whipping) cream

2 tbsp icing sugar

¹/₃ cup (80ml) passionfruit pulp

meringue frosting

²/₃ cup (150g) caster sugar

1 tbsp glucose syrup

2 tbsp water

3 egg whites

1 tbsp caster sugar, extra

TIP

You can make the cakes a day ahead. Complete the recipe to the end of step 5 then refrigerate for several hours or overnight. Cover the cake with the meringue frosting up to 3 hours before serving.

1 Preheat oven to 160°C (140°C fan/325°F/Gas 3). Grease two deep 20cm round cake pans; line the bottoms and sides with baking paper, extending the paper 5cm above the edge.

2 Beat the butter, sugar, and vanilla extract in a large bowl with an electric mixer until light and fluffy. Beat in the eggs, one at a time. Fold in the sifted flours and milk, in two batches. Divide the mixture into the pans.

3 Bake the cakes for 1 hour 25 minutes or until a skewer inserted into the centre comes out clean. Leave in the pans for 5 minutes before turning, top-side down, onto wire racks to cool.

4 Meanwhile, make the passionfruit cream. Beat the cream in a small bowl with an electric mixer until soft peaks form. Stir in the sifted icing sugar and passionfruit pulp.

5 Split the cold cakes in half. Spread one cake layer with one-third of the passionfruit cream, top with one-quarter of the raspberries, then with another cake layer. Repeat layering, finishing with a cake layer.

6 Make the meringue frosting. Stir the sugar, glucose syrup, and water in a small saucepan over a medium heat until the sugar dissolves. Bring to the boil; boil for 3 minutes or until the syrup reaches 116°C on a sugar thermometer (or when a teaspoon of syrup dropped into a cup of cold water forms a soft ball when the mixture is gathered up and rolled between your fingers). Remove from the heat to allow the bubbles to subside. Meanwhile, beat the egg whites in a small bowl with an electric mixer until soft peaks form; beat in the extra sugar until dissolved. With the motor operating, pour in the hot syrup in a thin steady stream; beat on high speed for 5 minutes or until the mixture is thick and cool.

7 Spread the frosting over the top and side of the cake; decorate the cake with the remaining raspberries.

Baked chocolate caramel cheesecake

PREP + COOK TIME **1 HOUR 40 MINUTES + REFRIGERATION AND COOLING** | SERVES **16**

Swap butternut snap biscuits for plain or chocolate biscuits if you prefer. If you use another type of biscuit, add enough extra melted butter until the crumbs come together. Serve the cheesecake topped with whipped cream or ice-cream and grated chocolate.

250g butternut snap biscuits (or plain or chocolate biscuits), broken into pieces

80g unsalted butter, melted

1/3 cup (80ml) pure (single) cream

100g dark chocolate, finely chopped

500g cream cheese, at room temperature

2/3 cup (150g) caster sugar

2 tsp vanilla bean paste

3 eggs

2/3 cup (160g) sour cream

380g canned caramel or dulce de leche

1   Grease a deep 22cm round cake pan; line the bottom and side with baking paper, extending the paper 5cm over the side.

2   Process the biscuits until fine. Add the butter; process until combined. Press the mixture evenly over the base of the pan. Refrigerate for 30 minutes.

3   Meanwhile, heat the cream in a small saucepan over a low heat for 1 minute or until hot but not boiling. Remove from heat; stir in the chocolate until melted. Cool for 15 minutes.

4   Preheat oven to 160°C (140°C fan/325°F/Gas 3). Beat the cream cheese, sugar, and vanilla paste in a medium bowl with an electric mixer until smooth (do not overbeat). Beat in the eggs, one at a time, until combined; beat in the sour cream.

5   Spread half the caramel over the biscuit base. Pour the cream cheese mixture over the caramel. Drop spoonfuls of the chocolate mixture and remaining caramel onto the cream cheese mixture. Use a bamboo skewer to swirl the mixtures together.

6   Bake for 50 minutes or until just set around the edge, but still slightly wobbly in the centre. Cool the cheesecake in the oven with door ajar. Refrigerate for 4 hours or overnight. Stand at room temperature for 30 minutes before serving.

TIPS

- Whisk the caramel before using.
- Use a hot dry knife to cut the cheesecake, wiping the blade clean between cuts.
- The cheesecake can be made a day ahead; keep covered, in the fridge.

Flourless chocolate cake

PREP + COOK TIME **1 HOUR + COOLING AND STANDING** | SERVES **12**

This gluten-free chocolate cake cuts out the flour but none of the flavour. Warm and gooey on the inside, coffee and hazelnuts bring a delicious depth to this chocolatey treat. Serve dusted in cocoa powder with a side of vanilla cream.

175g unsalted butter, chopped

200g dark chocolate (70% cocoa), coarsely chopped

½ cup (50g) cocoa powder, plus extra to dust

1 tbsp instant coffee granules

1 tbsp boiling water

6 eggs, at room temperature

1½ cups (330g) raw caster sugar

2 cups (200g) hazelnut meal

vanilla bean cream

300ml thickened (whipping) cream

1 teaspoon vanilla bean paste

2 tsp icing sugar

1 Preheat oven to 180°C/350°F. Grease a deep 22cm round springform pan; line the bottom and side with baking paper.

2 Place the butter, chocolate, and cocoa powder in a large heatproof bowl over a medium saucepan of simmering water (make sure the base of the bowl doesn't touch the water). Stir until the butter and chocolate melt and the mixture is smooth. Remove the bowl from the heat; cool for 15 minutes.

3 Meanwhile, combine the coffee and the boiling water in a small heatproof jug. Beat the eggs and sugar in a small bowl with an electric mixer for 2 minutes or until thick and creamy. Stir in the coffee mixture. Add the egg mixture to the chocolate mixture; stir until just combined. Fold in the hazelnut meal. Pour the mixture into the pan.

4 Bake the cake for 45 minutes or until a skewer inserted into the centre comes out clean. Leave the cake in the pan for 30 minutes.

5 Meanwhile, make the vanilla bean cream. Beat the cream, vanilla paste, and sugar in a medium bowl with an electric mixer until soft peaks form.

6 Just before serving, dust the cake with extra cocoa powder, and serve with the vanilla bean cream.

Honey and fig tiramisu cake

PREP + COOK TIME **1 HOUR + REFRIGERATION** | SERVES **8**

Classic tiramisu flavours are enhanced with figs and honey to transform this traditional
Italian dessert into a sweet masterpiece. You will need to start this recipe a day ahead and
the liqueur can be omitted, if you prefer.

2 medium oranges (480g)

4 egg yolks

¹/₂ cup (110g) caster sugar

¹/₄ cup (90g) honey, plus extra to drizzle

500g mascarpone

300ml thickened (whipping) cream

¹/₄ cup (60ml) hazelnut-flavoured liqueur

450g plain sponge cake (2 round cakes)

50g dark chocolate, shaved

¹/₄ cup (35g) coarsely chopped roasted hazelnuts

6 figs (360g), halved or quartered

1 Grease an 8cm deep, 18cm round springform pan; line the bottom and side with three layers of baking paper, extending the papers 5cm above the edge.

2 Finely grate 2 teaspoons of rind from the oranges. Squeeze the juice from the oranges; you will need ¹/₂ cup (125ml) of juice.

3 Beat the egg yolks, sugar, honey, and grated rind in a small bowl with an electric mixer for 5 minutes or until thick and creamy. Transfer the mixture to a medium bowl; fold in three-quarters of the mascarpone. Beat the cream in a medium bowl with an electric mixer until firm peaks form; fold gently into the mascarpone mixture.

4 Combine the orange juice and liqueur in a medium bowl.

5 Split the cakes in half. Place one cake layer inside the pan. Drizzle with a quarter of the juice mixture. Spread with a quarter of the mascarpone mixture. Repeat layering, finishing with the mascarpone mixture. Cover; refrigerate overnight.

6 Release the cake from the pan and remove the paper. Just before serving, sprinkle with the shaved chocolate and hazelnuts; top with the figs and drizzle with extra honey.

Passionfruit and lemon syrup cake

PREP + COOK TIME **1 HOUR 30 MINUTES** | SERVES **8**

This cake is a flavour sensation bringing richness, tart fruitiness, and satisfying sweetness to the palate. Serve warm from the oven drizzled in hot passionfruit syrup, with a swirl of fresh cream or a scoop of ice-cream on the side, if you like.

²/₃ cup (160ml) passionfruit pulp (reserve the juice and seeds)

250g butter, softened

1 tbsp finely grated lemon rind

1 cup (220g) caster sugar

3 eggs

³/₄ cup (180ml) buttermilk

reserved passionfruit juice

2 cups (300g) self-raising flour

lemon syrup

³/₄ cup (165g) caster sugar

¹/₃ cup (80ml) lemon juice

¹/₄ cup (60ml) water

reserved passionfruit seeds

1   Preheat oven to 180°C (160°C fan/350°F/Gas 4). Grease and lightly flour a 24cm bundt pan (see tip).

2   Strain the passionfruit over a medium jug; reserve the juice for the cake mixture, and the seeds for the lemon syrup.

3   Beat the butter, lemon rind, and sugar in a small bowl with an electric mixer until light and fluffy. Beat in the eggs, one at a time. Transfer the mixture to a large bowl; fold in the combined buttermilk and reserved passionfruit juice, and the sifted flour in two batches. Pour the mixture into the pan.

4   Bake the cake for 1 hour or until a skewer inserted into the centre comes out clean. Leave the cake in the pan for 5 minutes before turning onto a wire rack placed over a tray.

5   Meanwhile, make the lemon syrup. Place the sugar, lemon juice, the water, and half the reserved passionfruit seeds (discard the remaining seeds or freeze for another use) in a small saucepan; stir over a medium heat, without boiling, until the sugar dissolves. Simmer, uncovered, without stirring, for 5 minutes.

6   Pour the hot syrup over the hot cake; serve the cake warm.

TIP

You can also make the cake in a greased and lined deep 22cm round cake pan or a buttered and floured 21cm baba cake pan.

PIES
AND TARTS

Here you'll find a wonderful array of sweet
and savoury bakes, from elegant dessert
tarts through to golden topped classic pies
perfect for serving on a winter's night.

Mini macadamia, pecan, and walnut pies

PREP + COOK TIME **50 MINUTES + REFRIGERATION** | MAKES **6**

Macadamias, pecans, and walnuts bring a nutty crunch to these scrumptious sticky-sweet tarts. Enjoy these warm, toasted, syrupy flavours for morning or afternoon tea, or serve as a dessert with a scoop of ice-cream on the side.

3 sheets shortcrust pastry

$^1/_3$ cup (50g) raw macadamias

$^1/_3$ cup (45g) pecans

$^1/_3$ cup (35g) walnuts

2 tbsp brown sugar

1 tbsp plain flour

40g butter, melted

2 eggs, lightly beaten

$^3/_4$ cup (180ml) maple syrup (see tips)

1 Grease six 10cm round loose-based fluted tart tins.

2 Cut each pastry sheet in half diagonally. Lift the pastry into the tins. Press into the bottoms and sides; trim the edges. Cover; refrigerate for 30 minutes.

3 Meanwhile, preheat oven to 200°C (180°C fan/400°F/Gas 6).

4 Place the tins on an oven tray. Line the pastry in each tin with baking paper; fill with dried beans or rice. Bake for 10 minutes. Remove paper and beans; bake for a further 7 minutes or until lightly browned.

5 Meanwhile, combine the remaining ingredients in a bowl.

6 Reduce oven temperature to 180°C (160°C fan/350°F/Gas 4).

7 Divide the filling among the pastry cases. Bake the pies for 20 minutes or until set. Cool.

TIPS

• Make sure you use pure maple syrup in the nut filling; maple-flavoured syrup is not an adequate substitute for the real thing.

• Pies can be served warm with ice-cream or at room temperature.

Nectarine and almond tart

PREP + COOK TIME **1 HOUR 45 MINUTES + REFRIGERATION AND COOLING** | SERVES **12**

Almond frangipane and soft, juicy nectarines in a rich, buttery, melt-in-your-mouth pastry
case make this tart a delectable dessert. Serve straight from the oven drizzled in warm honey
and with a side serving of ice-cream, if you like.

1¹/₃ cups (200g) plain flour

125g cold unsalted butter, chopped

2 tbsp iced water, approximately

450g nectarines

2 tbsp flaked almonds

2 tbsp honey, warmed

almond frangipane

120g unsalted butter, softened

¹/₂ cup (110g) caster sugar

2 eggs

2 tbsp plain flour

1 cup (120g) almond meal

1 Sift the flour into a large bowl; rub in the butter with your fingertips until
the mixture resembles coarse breadcrumbs. Mix in enough of the water
to make the ingredients just come together. Knead the dough on a lightly
floured surface until smooth. Flatten the dough slightly, wrap in plastic
wrap (cling film); refrigerate for 20 minutes.

2 Grease a 22cm round loose-based tart tin. Roll the pastry on a lightly
floured surface, or between sheets of baking paper, until large enough
to line the tin.

3 Lift the pastry into the tin; press over the bottom and side, trim excess
pastry. Prick the base all over with a fork. Refrigerate for 20 minutes.

4 Preheat oven to 200°C (180°C fan/400°F/Gas 6).

5 Place the tart tin on an oven tray, line the pastry with baking paper; fill
with dried beans or rice. Bake for 15 minutes. Remove the paper and
beans; bake for a further 10 minutes or until the pastry is lightly browned
and crisp.

6 Meanwhile, make the almond frangipane. Beat the butter and sugar in
a medium bowl with an electric mixer until light and fluffy. Beat in the
eggs, one at a time, until combined. Stir in the sifted flour and the
almond meal.

7 Cut the nectarines in half; remove the stones. Cut the nectarines into
wedges. Spoon the frangipane into the tart shell; top with the nectarines,
cut-side up, pushing them lightly into the frangipane. Sprinkle with the
flaked almonds.

8 Bake the tart for 45 minutes or until golden; cool the tart in the pan.
Serve the tart drizzled with warmed honey.

Spiced cherry and apple pies

PREP + COOK TIME **1 HOUR** | MAKES **6**

These delicious traditional autumnal pies will bring warmth and nostalgic comfort to your table. You can use Granny Smith or Golden Delicious apples for this recipe as they both hold their shape well after cooking.

800g green apples

³/₄ cup (165g) caster sugar

2 tbsp water

1 tsp mixed spice

500g frozen pitted cherries

3 sheets frozen shortcrust pastry, just thawed

1 egg yolk, lightly beaten with 1 tbsp water

300ml thick (double) cream

1 Preheat oven to 200°C (180°C fan/400°F/Gas 6).

2 Peel, core, and cut the apples into chunks. Place in a large saucepan with the sugar, water, and mixed spice; cook, stirring, over a medium heat, until the sugar dissolves. Cover; cook for 10 minutes or until the apple is just tender.

3 Stir the cherries into the apple; cook, covered, for 3 minutes or until the cherries are soft but still hold their shape.

4 Using one of six 11cm, 1-cup (250ml) pie dishes, cut out two rounds from each sheet of pastry, tracing around the upturned dish with a small knife. Reserve the pastry scraps, if you like, to decorate the pie tops in step 5. Using a slotted spoon, transfer the fruit from the syrup into all six dishes; reserve the syrup.

5 Place the pastry rounds over the fruit filling; press the edges to seal. Brush the pastry tops with the egg mixture; cut a slit in the centres. If you like, use the reserved pastry scraps to make decorations (any shapes of your choice) to top your pies.

6 Place the pie dishes on an oven tray. Bake for 25 minutes or until the pastry is golden. Serve warm with cream and the reserved syrup.

TIPS

Decorating ideas:

• Crimping – Using the tines of a fork, crimp around the rim of the pies.

• Lattice – Cut pastry into narrow strips using a floured pastry wheel. Weave the pastry strips directly over the pie filling.

• Frilled edge – Using your fingers, pinch the edge of the pastry together to form a frilled edge.

Lemon tart

PREP + COOK TIME **1 HOUR 30 MINUTES + REFRIGERATION** | SERVES **8**

Classic lemon tart makes an elegant dessert. Dust with icing sugar and decorate with raspberries, if you like. This tart tastes even better if made the day before serving; keep, covered, in the fridge.

1¼ cups (185g) plain flour

¼ cup (40g) icing sugar

¼ cup (30g) almond meal

125g (4oz) cold butter, chopped

1 egg yolk

1 tbsp icing sugar, extra

lemon filling

1 tbsp finely grated lemon rind

½ cup (125ml) lemon juice

5 eggs

¾ cup (165g) caster sugar

1 cup (250ml) thickened (whipping) cream

1   Process the flour, icing sugar, almond meal, and butter until combined. Add the egg yolk; process until the ingredients just come together. Knead the dough on a lightly floured surface until smooth. Wrap in plastic wrap (cling film); refrigerate for 30 minutes.

2   Roll the pastry out between sheets of baking paper until large enough to line a 25.5cm round loose-based fluted tart tin. Ease the pastry onto the bottom and side; trim the edge. Cover; refrigerate for 30 minutes.

3   Meanwhile, preheat oven to 200°C (180°C fan/400°F/Gas 6).

4   Place the tart tin on an oven tray. Line the pastry case with baking paper, fill with dried beans or rice. Bake for 15 minutes. Remove the paper and beans; bake for a further 15 minutes or until lightly browned. Reduce oven to 180°C (160°C fan/350°F/Gas 4).

5   Meanwhile, make the lemon filling. Whisk the ingredients in a medium bowl until combined; stand for 5 minutes.

6   Pour the filling into the pastry case. Bake the tart for 30 minutes or until the filling has set slightly; cool.

7   Refrigerate the tart until cold. Serve dusted with extra sifted icing sugar.

TIP

You will need 3 medium lemons (420g) for this tart.

Peach and raspberry tarts

PREP + COOK TIME **40 MINUTES** | SERVES **8**

This stunning fruity and fresh tart makes a beautiful dessert. Serve with cream or ice-cream, if you like. We used a combination of yellow-flesh and white-flesh peaches; you could use just yellow, if you prefer.

60g butter, softened

1/3 cup (75g) caster sugar

1 egg

1/2 tsp orange blossom water

3/4 cup (75g) almond meal

2 tbsp plain flour

8 sheets filo pastry

100g butter, melted

5 medium peaches (750g), sliced

150g raspberries

1/4 cup (35g) coarsely chopped pistachios

1/4 cup (90g) honey

1 Beat the butter and sugar in a small bowl with an electric mixer until creamy. Beat in the egg and orange blossom water until combined. Stir in the almond meal and flour.

2 Preheat oven to 180°C (160°C fan/350°F/Gas 4). Line two oven trays with baking paper.

3 Brush one sheet of filo pastry with a little of the melted butter; top with another pastry sheet and brush again. Repeat the layering and brushing with the remaining pastry and butter. Cut the pastry stack in half lengthways. Place the pastry stacks on the oven trays. Spread the almond mixture on the pastry, leaving a 1cm border.

4 Bake the tarts for 20 minutes or until browned and the pastry is cooked underneath.

5 Serve the tarts topped with the peaches, raspberries, and pistachios; drizzle with honey.

TIP

Unravel the packet of filo pastry and place 8 sheets stacked together aside; cover with plastic wrap (cling film) and a damp tea towel. Place the remaining pastry, wrapped in plastic wrap, back in the pack and refrigerate. Pull sheets off one at time.

Rhubarb galette

PREP + COOK TIME **30 MINUTES** | SERVES **4**

Galettes consist of a pastry base, topped with either sweet or savoury fillings, with edges that are roughly folded in to create a gorgeous, rustic, relaxed-looking bake. Here we've used tangy rhubarb as our filling. Serve with cream, if you like.

20g butter, melted

275g coarsely chopped rhubarb

1/3 cup (75g) firmly packed brown sugar

1 tsp finely grated orange rind

1 sheet frozen ready-rolled puff pastry, just thawed

2 tbsp almond meal

10g butter, melted, extra

2 tbsp honey

2 tsp icing sugar

thick (double) cream, to serve

1 Preheat oven to 220°C (200°C fan/425°F/Gas 7). Line an oven tray with baking paper.

2 Place the butter, rhubarb, sugar, and orange rind in a medium bowl; toss until well coated.

3 Cut a 24cm round from the pastry sheet, place on the lined oven tray; sprinkle the almond meal evenly over the pastry. Spread the rhubarb mixture on the pastry, leaving a 4cm border; fold the pastry border up and around the filling. Brush the edge with the extra melted butter.

4 Bake the galette for 20 minutes or until lightly browned. Brush the warm galette with honey. Just before serving, dust with icing sugar.

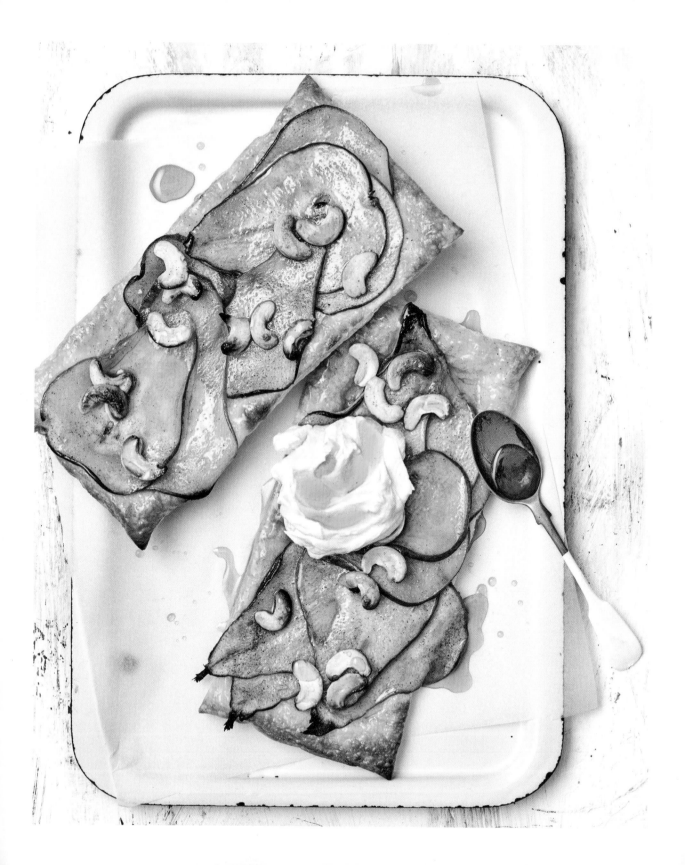

Pear, maple, and cashew tarts

PREP + COOK TIME **30 MINUTES** | SERVES **4**

Maple syrup glazed pears on a golden base of puff pastry with the added crunch of cashews
and the warm hug of cinnamon make this a dessert of dreams. Serve with Greek yogurt
instead of labneh, if you like.

1 large pear (330g)

1 sheet puff pastry

20g butter, melted

1/4 cup (60ml) pure maple syrup

1/4 cup (40g) cashews, halved

2 tsp cinnamon sugar (see tips)

1 cup (280g) labneh (see tips)

1 Preheat oven to 220°C (200°C fan/425°F/Gas 7). Grease a large oven tray;
   line with baking paper.

2 Using a mandolin, V-slicer, or sharp knife, thinly slice the unpeeled
   pear lengthways.

3 Cut the pastry sheet in half lengthways; place on the oven tray. Arrange
   the pear on the pastry. Brush with the butter and half the syrup. Top with
   the cashews and half the cinnamon sugar.

4 Bake the tarts for 20 minutes or until the pastry is browned.

5 Meanwhile, combine the labneh with the remaining cinnamon sugar
   in a small bowl.

6 Drizzle the remaining syrup over the tarts while they are still hot; serve
   with the cinnamon labneh.

TIPS

- If you can't find cinnamon sugar, you can make
your own by combining 1 teaspoon of caster sugar
with 1 teaspoon of ground cinnamon.
- Labneh is a strained yogurt cheese, available
from some supermarkets and delicatessens.

Mince pies

PREP + COOK TIME **1 HOUR + REFRIGERATION** | MAKES **12**

You will need to make this recipe a month ahead if you're not using store-bought fruit mince.
The three-in-one basic fruit mix is also enough to make a regular-sized cake or a pudding –
boiled or steamed – to serve ten people.

1 cup (150g) plain flour

1 tbsp icing sugar

75g cold butter, coarsely chopped

1 egg, separated

1 tbsp iced water, approximately

1 cup three-in-one basic fruit mix (recipe below)
or store-bought fruit mince

1 tsp finely grated lemon rind

1 tbsp white (granulated) sugar

three-in-one basic fruit mix

2^{1}/$_{3}$ cups (375g) sultanas

2 cups (320g) currants

2^{1}/$_{3}$ cups (375g) coarsely chopped raisins

1 cup (150g) finely chopped pitted dates

^{2}/$_{3}$ cup (120g) finely chopped pitted prunes

1 cup (200g) finely chopped dried figs

2 large apples (400g), coarsely grated

^{1}/$_{4}$ cup (90g) golden syrup or treacle

2 cups (440g) firmly packed dark brown sugar

1^{1}/$_{2}$ cups (375ml) brandy

2 tsp ground ginger

1 tsp ground nutmeg

1 tsp ground cinnamon

1 Make the three-in-one basic fruit mix. Combine the ingredients in a large bowl; cover tightly with plastic wrap (cling film). Store in a cool, dark place for a month (or longer, if desired) before using. Stir the mixture every two or three days. Makes 9 cups (2.5kg).

2 Grease a 12-hole (2-tbsp/40ml) round-based patty pan.

3 Process the flour, icing sugar, and butter until crumbly. Add the egg yolk and enough of the water to make the ingredients just come together. Knead the dough on a lightly floured surface until smooth. Cover the dough with plastic wrap (cling film); refrigerate for 30 minutes.

4 Preheat oven to 200°C (180°C fan/400°F/Gas 6).

5 Roll two-thirds of the dough between sheets of baking paper until 3mm thick. Use the round cutter to cut 12 rounds from the pastry (re-roll the pastry scraps if necessary to make a total of 12 rounds). Press the rounds into the pan holes; reserve the pastry scraps.

6 Combine the basic fruit mix and lemon rind in a medium bowl. Drop a level tablespoon of fruit mince into each pastry case.

7 Combine the reserved pastry with any pastry scraps; roll out until 3mm thick. Using a star cutter, or a sharp knife, cut out 12 stars. Place the stars in the centre of the pies; brush with egg white, sprinkle with the white sugar. Bake for 20 minutes or until the pies are lightly browned. Stand for 5 minutes before transferring to a wire rack to cool. Serve dusted with extra icing sugar, if you like.

Spicy panforte

PREP + COOK TIME **1 HOUR 15 MINUTES + OVERNIGHT COOLING** | SERVES **12**

Panforte is a traditional Italian cake originating from the Tuscan city of Siena. Packed with fruit, honey, nuts, and spices it has an irresistibly chewy texture and is a favourite festive dessert in Italy. It also makes a great homemade Christmas gift.

1 medium orange (240g)

1/2 cup (75g) plain flour

1 tbsp mixed spice

2 tsp ground cardamom

1 tsp freshly ground black pepper

1/3 cup (40g) almond meal

1 cup (120g) skinless hazelnuts, roasted

1/2 cup (50g) walnut halves, roasted

1/2 cup (70g) pistachios, roasted lightly

1/2 cup (125g) coarsely chopped glacé apricots

1/2 cup (65g) dried sweetened cranberries

1/2 cup (110g) crystallised ginger

100g white chocolate, coarsely chopped

1/2 cup (110g) caster sugar

1/2 cup (175g) honey

1 tbsp water

1 tbsp icing sugar

1 Preheat oven to 160°C (140°C fan/325°F/Gas 3). Line the bottom and side of a 20cm springform pan with baking paper.

2 Remove rind from the orange with a zester. (Or peel the orange thinly with a vegetable peeler, avoiding any white pith. Cut the rind into long thin strips.)

3 Sift the flour and spices into a large bowl. Stir in the orange rind, almond meal, nuts, fruit, ginger, and chocolate.

4 Stir the caster sugar, honey, and water in a small saucepan over a medium heat until the sugar dissolves. Simmer for 2 minutes or until a cooking thermometer reaches 116°C (or when a teaspoon of syrup, dropped into a cup of cold water, forms a soft ball when the mixture is gathered up and rolled between your fingers). Add the sugar syrup to the flour mixture; stir well. Press the mixture firmly into the pan; smooth the surface.

5 Bake the panforte for 45 minutes or until it comes away slightly from the edge of the pan. Leave the panforte in the pan overnight to cool. Just before serving, dust with icing sugar. Cut into thin wedges.

TIPS

- Roasting nuts brings out the flavour. Spread nuts onto an oven tray, roast in 180°C (160°C fan/350°F/ Gas 4) oven for 5 minutes, or until nuts are golden.
- Panforte can be made up to 2 weeks ahead; store in an airtight container at room temperature.

Freeform beetroot and hazelnut tart

PREP + COOK TIME **1 HOUR** | SERVES **6**

Creamy ricotta and earthy beetroot are combined in this savoury rustic tart that replaces a traditional pastry base with a nutritious sweet potato crust. Perfect for an al fresco lunch or light supper, the tart is delicious served warm or at room temperature.

2 x 250g packets vacuum-packed cooked beetroot

1 tbsp fresh thyme leaves

2 tbsp red wine vinegar

2½ tbsp extra virgin olive oil

salt and freshly ground black pepper

700g sweet potatoes, coarsely chopped

1½ cups (150g) hazelnut meal

1 egg, lightly beaten

½ cup (65g) grated gruyère cheese

1 large red onion (300g), cut into thin wedges

40g baby spinach leaves

⅓ cup (45g) skinless roasted hazelnuts, coarsely chopped

ricotta cream

1½ cups (360g) soft ricotta (see tips)

2 tsp finely grated lemon rind

1 tbsp lemon juice

2 garlic cloves, crushed

1 Preheat oven to 200°C (180°C fan/400°F/Gas 6). Line a large oven tray and a small oven tray with baking paper.

2 Cut the beetroot into wedges; toss in a bowl with the thyme, vinegar, and 2 tablespoons of the olive oil. Season with salt and pepper.

3 Boil or steam the sweet potato for 10 minutes or until soft; drain well. Place the sweet potato in a large bowl; mash until smooth. Stir in the hazelnut meal, egg, and cheese; season with salt and pepper. Spread the mixture on the large tray into a 28cm x 36cm rectangle, about 1cm thick.

4 Bake the tart base for 30 minutes or until set and the edges are golden.

5 Meanwhile, place the onion on the small oven tray; drizzle with the remaining olive oil. Roast in the oven for the last 15 minutes of tart base baking time or until the onion is tender and golden.

6 Meanwhile, make the ricotta cream. Whisk the ingredients in a large bowl until smooth and well combined; season with salt and pepper to taste.

7 Spread the ricotta cream over the base. Top with the beetroot, roasted onion, spinach leaves, and hazelnuts; drizzle with the remaining dressing from the beetroot mixture. Season with salt and pepper.

TIPS

- You can use cottage cheese instead of ricotta.
- The sweet potato tart base can be made several hours ahead.

Apple and brie tart

PREP + COOK TIME **45 MINUTES** | SERVES **4**

Brie and apple are the perfect pairing in this flaky, golden tart, which would make a perfect twist on a cheese course for a dinner party. Alternatively, serve it for lunch with a bitter-leaf salad on the side.

2 sheets puff pastry

100g brie

2 tsp honey

20g butter

2 medium green apples (300g) (see tip)

1/4 cup (25g) coarsely chopped walnuts

2 tsp chopped fresh chives

1 Preheat oven to 220°C (200°C fan/425°F/Gas 7). Line an oven tray with baking paper.

2 Carefully remove the backing plastic from the pastry sheets, then stack them on top of one another. Roll them out on a lightly floured sheet of baking paper into a 34cm square; cut out a 34cm circle, discard the pastry scraps. Place the pastry round on the lined tray; prick all over with a fork. Cover with a sheet of baking paper, then another oven tray. Bake for 10 minutes. Remove the top tray and baking paper; bake for a further 10 minutes.

3 Meanwhile, thinly slice three-quarters of the brie; finely chop the remaining brie.

4 Combine the honey and butter in a small microwave-safe bowl; microwave on HIGH (100%) until melted. Core the unpeeled apples; slice thinly crossways into rounds.

5 Top the pastry base with the sliced brie then the sliced apple; brush the apple with the honey mixture. Top with the walnuts and chopped brie.

6 Bake the tart for a further 15 minutes. Leave on the tray for 5 minutes before serving sprinkled with chives.

TIP

Use a mandolin or V-slicer to cut the unpeeled apples into thin slices; slice them at the last moment to avoid the apples discolouring.

Roast vegetable filo tart

PREP + COOK TIME **1 HOUR 10 MINUTES + COOLING** | SERVES **6**

Roasted vegetables and feta sit on a crispy filo pastry base making this a light tart, bursting with colour, nutrition, and flavour. Serve sprinkled with fresh basil leaves and a mixed green leaf salad on the side, if you like.

6 medium roma (plum) tomatoes (450g), quartered

1 small red onion (100g), thickly sliced

2 small red capsicums (peppers) (300g)

2 small yellow capsicums (peppers) (300g)

100g feta, crumbled

1 tbsp finely shredded fresh basil

9 sheets filo pastry

cooking-oil spray

1 Preheat oven to 220°C (200°C fan/425°F/Gas 7).

2 Combine the tomato and onion in a medium baking dish. Roast for 30 minutes or until the onion is soft. Remove from the oven; cool.

3 Reduce oven to 200°C (180°C fan/400°F/Gas 6).

4 Meanwhile, preheat the grill. Quarter the capsicums; discard seeds and membranes. Roast under a hot grill, skin-side up, until the skin blisters and blackens. Remove from the grill; cover the capsicum with baking paper for 5 minutes. Peel away the skin; slice the capsicum thinly. Place the capsicum, feta, and basil in a baking dish with the tomato mixture; stir gently to combine.

5 Stack all nine sheets of filo on an oven tray, spraying every third sheet with cooking-oil spray. Fold all four sides of the filo stack in slightly to form an 18cm x 30cm rectangular tart shell. Fill the shell with the vegetable mixture; bake for 15 minutes or until the pastry is golden.

Pork and apple sausage rolls

PREP + COOK TIME **35 MINUTES** | MAKES **6**

Perfect for a light supper or a warming snack on a chilly day, these golden sausage rolls are best eaten warm straight from the oven. Serve with an apple and celery salad, dressed with a little olive oil and lemon juice, if you like.

1 green apple (150g), skin on

600g minced pork and veal mixture

1 cup (60g) finely grated parmesan

1 cup (50g) fresh breadcrumbs

1 tbsp Dijon mustard

2 tbsp finely chopped fresh thyme

2 eggs

salt and freshly ground black pepper

3 sheets frozen puff pastry, just thawed

1 tsp fresh thyme leaves, extra

sriracha chilli sauce, to serve

1 Preheat oven to 220°C (200°C fan/425°F/Gas 7). Grease and line a large oven tray with baking paper.

2 Grate the unpeeled apple; squeeze any excess moisture from the flesh. Combine the mince, parmesan, breadcrumbs, grated apple, mustard, thyme, and 1 lightly beaten egg in a medium bowl; season with salt and pepper.

3 Lightly beat the remaining egg in a small bowl. Place 1 sheet of pastry on a work surface. Place one-third of the filling mixture lengthways down one side of the pastry, 1.5cm from the edge. Brush the pastry edge with a little egg; roll to form a sausage roll. Trim and discard the excess pastry. Repeat with the remaining pastry and filling mixture and a little more egg. Cut each roll in half.

4 Place the rolls, seam-side down, on the lined baking tray; brush the tops with egg and sprinkle with extra thyme.

5 Bake the rolls for 25 minutes or until the pastry is golden and the rolls are cooked through. Serve with sriracha.

Tomato and goat's cheese tart with rice and seed crust

PREP + COOK TIME **1 HOUR 10 MINUTES + COOLING** | SERVES **4**

This gluten-free tart replaces pastry with a brown rice dough. Using pre-cooked rice and with no rolling required, the crust is super easy to make and results in a delicious golden casing with an added crunch that perfectly complements the soft creamy goat's cheese.

500g packaged ready-cooked brown basmati rice

$^1/_3$ cup (50g) sunflower seeds

$1^1/_2$ cups (120g) finely grated parmesan

3 eggs

1 tsp sea salt flakes

500g fresh ricotta

150g soft goat's cheese

$^1/_4$ cup (60ml) milk

1 tbsp wholegrain mustard

1 garlic clove, finely chopped

400g mixed tomatoes, halved and sliced

2 tbsp small fresh basil leaves

1 tbsp extra virgin olive oil

2 tsp balsamic vinegar

Freshly ground black pepper

1 Preheat oven to 200°C (180°C fan/400°F/Gas 6). Grease a 24cm springform pan.

2 Process the rice, seeds, and half the parmesan until the rice is finely chopped. Add 1 egg and half the salt; process until coarse.

3 Using damp hands, press one-third of the rice dough over the bottom of the pan and the remaining two-thirds of the dough up the side of the pan, stopping 5mm from the top.

4 Bake the crust for 25 minutes or until golden and dry to the touch.

5 Meanwhile, process the ricotta, goat's cheese, milk, mustard, and garlic with the remaining parmesan, eggs, and salt until smooth.

6 Pour the cheese mixture into the warm rice crust. Reduce oven to 180°C (160°C fan/350°F/Gas 4); bake the tart for a further 30 minutes or until a skewer inserted into the centre comes out clean. Leave to cool for 1 hour.

7 Just before serving, arrange the tomatoes and basil on top of the tart; drizzle with the oil and vinegar. Season with freshly ground black pepper.

Easy cheesy leek quiche

PREP + COOK TIME **1 HOUR 20 MINUTES** | SERVES **6**

This golden quiche is perfect for lunch or a light supper. If you prefer, use trimmed fat asparagus spears instead of the leeks. Serve with bitter salad leaves tossed with sunflower seeds, pumpkin seeds, lemon juice, and olive oil.

2 sheets puff pastry

10 pencil leeks (180g) (see tips)

2 tsp olive oil

4 eggs

1 cup (250ml) single cream

1/2 cup (40g) finely grated parmesan

salt and freshly ground black pepper

140g soft goat's cheese, crumbled

1 Preheat oven to 220°C (200°C fan/425°F/Gas 7). Grease a 21cm x 30cm ovenproof dish or shallow, rectangular loose-based fluted tart tin.

2 Overlap the pastry sheets slightly; press to join. Lift the pastry into the dish, press onto the bottom and sides; trim the excess pastry. Prick the base all over with a fork; place the dish on an oven tray. Line the pastry with baking paper; fill with dried beans or rice. Bake for 10 minutes. Remove the paper and beans; bake for a further 10 minutes or until the pastry is browned and crisp.

3 Meanwhile, heat a grill plate (or barbecue or frying pan) to a medium heat. Trim and wash the leeks; pat dry. Brush the leeks with oil; cook on the grill, turning, for 5 minutes or until tender.

4 Reduce oven to 200°C (180°C fan/400°F/Gas 6).

5 Whisk the eggs, cream, and parmesan in a large bowl; season well. Pour the egg mixture into the pastry case; top with the leeks and half the goat's cheese.

6 Bake the quiche for 30 minutes or until set and golden. Serve topped with the remaining goat's cheese.

TIPS

- Pencil leeks are also known as baby or tiny leeks; use thick green onions (spring onions) instead if you can't find them.
- Quiche is best made on the day of serving.

Quiche variations

Individual quiches are perfect portable fare, ideal for work or school lunches. Team up with a handful of salad leaves or steamed veggies for a light meal. Mix and match your favourite fillings with the basic egg mixture.

Blue cheese

PREP + COOK TIME **40 MINUTES** | MAKES **12**

Preheat oven to 180°C (160°C fan/350°F/Gas 4). Grease a 12-hole (2-tbsp/40ml) flat-based patty pan. Using a 7cm cutter, cut 12 rounds from 2 sheets of shortcrust pastry; press the rounds into the pan holes. Divide 150g crumbled soft blue cheese and 1 tablespoon of chopped fresh flat-leaf parsley among the pastry cases. Whisk 2 eggs with 1 tablespoon of milk in a jug, season with salt and pepper; pour into the pastry cases. Bake for 25 minutes or until the quiches are set and the pastry is lightly browned. Top with extra flat-leaf parsley.

Ham and corn

PREP + COOK TIME **40 MINUTES** | MAKES **12**

Preheat oven to 180°C (160°C fan/350°F/Gas 4). Grease a 12-hole (2-tbsp/40ml) flat-based patty pan. Using a 7cm cutter, cut 12 rounds from 2 sheets of shortcrust pastry; press the rounds into the pan holes. Divide 90g chopped leg ham and 125g drained canned corn kernels (sweetcorn) among the pastry cases. Whisk 2 eggs with 1 tablespoon of milk in a jug, season with salt and pepper; pour into the pastry cases. Bake for 25 minutes or until the quiches are set and the pastry is lightly browned. Cook 2 slices of prosciutto in a dry frying pan over a medium heat until crisp; crumble over the quiches.

Capsicum and goat's cheese

PREP + COOK TIME **40 MINUTES** | MAKES **12**

Preheat oven to 180°C (160°C fan/350°F/Gas 4). Drain a 285g jar of piquillo peppers; pat dry with paper towel, slice thinly. Heat 20g butter in a frying pan over a medium heat; cook the peppers, 1 clove of crushed garlic, and 2 teaspoons of thyme, stirring, for 5 minutes. Cool. Grease a 12-hole (2-tbsp/40ml) flat-based patty pan. Using a 7cm cutter, cut 12 rounds from 2 sheets of shortcrust pastry; press the rounds into the pan holes. Spoon the pepper mixture into the pastry cases. Whisk 2 eggs with 1 tablespoon of milk in a jug, season with salt and pepper; pour into the pastry cases. Top with 60g crumbled soft goat's cheese. Bake for 25 minutes or until set and the pastry is lightly browned.

Smoked salmon and asparagus

PREP + COOK TIME **40 MINUTES** | MAKES **12**

Preheat oven to 180°C (160°C fan/350°F/Gas 4). Grease a 12-hole (2-tbsp/40ml) flat-based patty pan. Using a 7cm cutter, cut 12 rounds from 2 sheets of shortcrust pastry; press the rounds into the pan holes. Divide 5 chopped asparagus spears (75g), 125g finely shredded smoked salmon, and 2 tablespoons of finely chopped fresh chives among the pastry cases. Whisk 3 eggs with 1 tablespoon of milk in a medium jug, season with salt and pepper; pour into the pastry cases. Top with ¼ cup (20g) finely grated parmesan. Bake for 25 minutes or until the quiches are set and the pastry is lightly browned.

Quinoa and kale tart

PREP + COOK TIME **1 HOUR 30 MINUTES + REFRIGERATION** | SERVES **6**

This nutrition-packed vegetarian tart boasts a gluten-free crust made of quinoa and parmesan, which is baked until crisp and golden. Serve for a light lunch topped with rocket leaves, dressed with lemon juice and olive oil.

³/₄ cup (150g) tri-coloured quinoa, rinsed

1¹/₂ cups (120g) finely grated parmesan

3 eggs

¹/₂ tsp salt flakes

1 tbsp olive oil

1 garlic clove, crushed

3 cups (70g) firmly packed coarsely chopped kale

¹/₄ cup (60ml) water

1 tbsp Dijon mustard

³/₄ cup (180ml) pure (single) cream

salt and freshly ground black pepper

1 Grease an 11cm x 35cm rectangular loose-based tart tin.

2 Cook the quinoa in a large saucepan of boiling water for 12 minutes or until tender; drain well. Cool. Process the quinoa and half the parmesan until the quinoa is finely chopped. Add 1 egg and half the salt; process until the mixture forms a coarse dough. Press the mixture evenly over the bottom and sides of the tart tin. Refrigerate for 30 minutes or until firm.

3 Meanwhile, preheat oven to 200°C (180°C fan/400°F/Gas 6).

4 Bake the tart shell for 30 minutes or until golden. Remove from the oven; reduce temperature to 180°C (160°C fan/350°F/Gas 4).

5 Meanwhile, heat the olive oil in a medium frying pan over a medium heat; cook the garlic for 30 seconds. Add the kale; cook, stirring, for 30 seconds. Add the water; cook, covered, for 3 minutes. Remove from the heat; stand, covered, for 1 minute. Cool; drain away any excess liquid.

6 Whisk the remaining eggs and half the remaining cheese with the mustard and cream in a medium bowl until combined; stir in the kale mixture and season with salt and pepper. Spread the mixture evenly into the tart shell; sprinkle with the remaining parmesan and salt.

7 Bake the tart for 30 minutes or until the filling is set.

Butter chicken hand pies

PREP + COOK TIME **40 MINUTES** | MAKES **4**

Indulge in a takeaway curry with a difference with these flaky golden pies that are rich with mildly spiced creamy chicken and fit perfectly in the palm of your hand. Ideal for snacking on the go or a casual light lunch with friends.

20g butter

1 small onion (80g), finely chopped

250g minced chicken

1 small carrot (70g), coarsely grated

2 tbsp butter chicken curry paste

2 tbsp frozen peas

salt and freshly ground black pepper

2 sheets puff pastry

1 egg, lightly beaten

1   Preheat oven to 220°C (200°C fan/425°F/Gas 7). Line a large oven tray with baking paper.

2   Melt the butter in a large frying pan over a medium-high heat; cook the onion, stirring, for 3 minutes or until soft. Add the chicken; cook, stirring, until browned. Add the carrot, curry paste, and peas; cook for 5 minutes or until thickened. Season with salt and pepper to taste.

3   Cut each pastry sheet into quarters (you will have eight squares). Place four of the pastry squares on the oven tray; divide the chicken filling evenly into the centre of the pastry squares. Brush the edges with egg.

4   Gently fold the remaining pastry squares in half; using kitchen scissors, cut three slits in the centre of the folded side. Open the pastry squares out; place them over the chicken filling. Press the pastry edges together; use a fork to seal them. Brush the top of the pies with egg.

5   Bake the pies for 25 minutes or until browned.

TIP

Combine ½ cup (140g) Greek yogurt with 2 tablespoons of finely chopped mint in a small bowl. Serve with the hand pies.

Beef and pea triangles

PREP + COOK TIME **40 MINUTES** | MAKES **12**

These tasty little samosa-style pastries are golden parcels of deliciousness perfect for
snacking, or turn them into a light meal by adding a fresh green salad on the side.
Serve with tomato sauce, if you like.

2 tsp olive oil

1 small onion (80g), finely chopped

1 garlic clove, crushed

500g minced beef

2 tbsp tomato paste

2/3 cup (170g) bottled passata

1/2 cup (60g) frozen peas

1/3 cup (7g) finely chopped fresh flat-leaf parsley

salt and freshly ground black pepper

3 sheets puff pastry

1 egg, lightly beaten

2 tsp poppy seeds

1 cup (250ml) tomato sauce (ketchup)

1 Preheat oven to 200°C (180°C fan/400°F/Gas 6). Line two large oven trays
   with baking paper.

2 Heat the olive oil in a large frying pan over a medium-high heat; cook
   the onion and garlic, stirring, for 3 minutes or until the onion softens.
   Increase the heat to high, add the beef; cook, stirring, for 5 minutes or
   until the beef is browned and cooked through. Add the tomato paste,
   passata, and peas; cook, stirring, until heated through. Remove from
   the heat; stir in the parsley. Season with salt and pepper to taste. Cool
   for 10 minutes.

3 Cut each pastry sheet into quarters (you will have 12 squares in total).
   Spoon even portions of the beef mixture into the centre of each square.
   Brush the edges with a little egg; fold the pastry in half diagonally to
   enclose the filling, pressing the edges together with a fork to seal.

4 Place the triangles on the oven trays; brush the top of the pastry with
   egg, sprinkle with poppy seeds. Bake for 15 minutes or until browned.
   Serve with tomato sauce.

TIP

Cooked triangles can be frozen for up to 3 months.

Chicken and leek pie

PREP + COOK TIME **1 HOUR 35 MINUTES + COOLING** | SERVES **6**

A hint of mustard cuts through the creamy filling of this chicken and leek pie, topped with golden flaky pastry. The perfect comforting winter warmer, serve for family lunches or dinner on chilly days.

2 cups (500ml) chicken stock

625g chicken breast fillets

60g butter

1 large leek (500g), thinly sliced

2 stalks celery (300g), trimmed, finely chopped

2 tbsp plain flour

2 tsp fresh thyme leaves

1/2 cup (125ml) milk

1 cup (250ml) pure (single) cream

2 tsp wholegrain mustard

salt and freshly ground black pepper

1 sheet puff pastry

1 egg yolk, lightly beaten

1 Bring the stock to the boil in a medium saucepan over a high heat. Add the chicken; return to the boil. Reduce the heat; simmer, covered, for 10 minutes or until the chicken is cooked. Remove from the heat; stand the chicken in the poaching liquid for 10 minutes. Remove the chicken; chop coarsely. Reserve 1 cup (250ml) of the poaching liquid; keep the remaining liquid for another use, or discard.

2 Heat the butter in a medium saucepan; cook the leek and celery, stirring, until the leek softens. Add the flour and thyme; cook, stirring, for 1 minute. Gradually stir in the reserved poaching liquid, milk, and cream; cook, stirring, until the mixture boils and thickens. Stir in the chopped chicken and mustard. Season with salt and pepper to taste. Cool for 15 minutes.

3 Preheat oven to 200°C (180°C fan/400°F/Gas 6). Oil a deep 6-cup (1.5-litre) pie or rectangular dish.

4 Spoon the chicken mixture into the dish; place the puff pastry over the filling, trim to fit the dish. Brush the pastry with egg yolk; cut two small slits in the top.

5 Bake the pie for 20 minutes or until puffed and browned. Serve sprinkled with extra thyme, if you like.

TIP

Pie filling can be made a day ahead. Store, covered, in the fridge until ready to use.

Silver beet and cheese snails

PREP + COOK TIME **1 HOUR** | SERVES **4**

These crispy filo pastry snails make a great lunch served with a green salad or roasted vegetables and could also be a fun way to get children to enjoy their greens. They are best baked just before eating and served warm from the oven.

750g silver beet (Swiss chard), trimmed, coarsely chopped

1 tbsp extra virgin olive oil

6 green onions (spring onions), thinly sliced

2 garlic cloves, crushed

1 cup (200g) cottage cheese

1/3 cup (16g) finely chopped fresh mint

1/3 cup (7g) finely chopped fresh flat-leaf parsley

2 egg yolks

salt and freshly ground black pepper

8 sheets filo pastry

1/4 cup (60ml) extra virgin olive oil, extra

2 tsp sesame seeds

1 tsp cumin seeds

1 Preheat oven to 180°C (160°C fan/350°F/Gas 4). Grease and line two oven trays with baking paper.

2 Cook the silver beet in a large saucepan of boiling water for 5 minutes; drain, rinse under cold water. Squeeze out excess water, place the silver beet in a large bowl.

3 Heat the olive oil in a medium frying pan over a low heat; cook the green onion and garlic, stirring occasionally, for 3 minutes or until soft. Add the onion mixture to the silver beet with the cottage cheese, herbs, and egg yolks; stir until well combined. Season with salt and pepper.

4 Brush one sheet of pastry with some of the extra oil, top with another sheet. Spoon one-quarter of the silver beet mixture along one long edge of the pastry and roll up tightly to form a log or sausage shape. Coil the pastry log into a snail shape. Place on the oven tray. Repeat with the remaining pastry and silver beet mixture to make 4 snails in total.

5 Brush each snail lightly with oil; sprinkle with the combined sesame and cumin seeds. Bake for 35 minutes or until the pastry is crisp and golden.

Garlicky pumpkin and feta quiches

PREP + COOK TIME **1 HOUR** | MAKES **6**

These tasty vegetarian quiches are so versatile – perfect for a midweek lunch or light dinner served with a bitter-leaf salad on the side, and any leftovers will make a great lunchbox addition the next day.

3 sheets shortcrust pastry

900g butternut pumpkin (butternut squash), peeled, chopped

3 garlic cloves, crushed

1/2 cup (125ml) pure (single) cream

1/4 cup (6g) coarsely chopped fresh sage

1/2 cup (60g) frozen peas

3 eggs, lightly beaten

salt and freshly ground black pepper

75g feta, crumbled

1 1/2 tbsp pine nuts

1/2 cup (140g) beetroot relish

1 Preheat oven to 200°C (180°C fan/400°F/Gas 6). Oil six 10cm x 13cm oval pie tins.

2 Cut each pastry sheet in half diagonally. Lift the pastry triangles into the tins; press into the sides, trim the edges.

3 Meanwhile, microwave the pumpkin on HIGH for 8 minutes or until tender. Transfer to a large bowl with the garlic; coarsely mash the pumpkin and garlic with a fork. Stir in the cream, sage, peas, and egg; season with salt and pepper.

4 Place the tins on an oven tray; line the pastry with baking paper, fill with dried beans or rice. Bake for 10 minutes. Remove the paper and beans; bake for a further 5 minutes or until lightly browned.

5 Fill the pastry cases with the pumpkin mixture. Sprinkle with crumbled feta and pine nuts. Bake for 25 minutes or until set and browned.

6 Serve the quiches topped with beetroot relish.

TIP

Quiches are suitable to freeze for up to 3 months. Defrost in the fridge overnight before reheating in a 180°C (160°C fan/350°F/Gas 4) oven.

Spring vegetable tart

PREP + COOK TIME **55 MINUTES + STANDING AND COOLING** | SERVES **6**

Beautiful spring vegetables bring colour and freshness to this vibrant tart that's perfect for
an al fresco lunch. Polenta varies in texture, from fine to coarse, depending on the brand.
For best results, use fine polenta for this recipe.

½ cup (85g) polenta

1½ cups (180g) almond meal

1 tbsp cumin seeds

1 tsp sea salt flakes

80g cold butter, chopped

1 tbsp iced water

1 egg white

1 small courgette (90g)

80g asparagus

⅓ cup (40g) frozen peas

2 tbsp small or micro mint leaves

tahini yogurt

1 cup (280g) Greek yogurt

¼ cup (70g) tahini

1 garlic clove, crushed

2 tsp lemon juice

salt and freshly ground black pepper

1   Preheat oven to 200°C (180°C fan/400°F/Gas 6). Grease an 11.5cm x 35cm rectangular loose-based tart tin.

2   Process the polenta, almond meal, cumin seeds, and salt until combined. Add the butter; pulse until the mixture resembles crumbs. Add the water and egg white; pulse until the mixture holds together when pinched, adding more iced water if needed. Press the mixture evenly over the bottom and sides of the tin, using the back of a wet spoon. Place the tin on an oven tray.

3   Bake the tart case for 30 minutes or until firm and lightly golden. Leave the tart in the tin for 15 minutes; carefully remove from the tin (the pastry will be fragile), transferring to a wire rack to cool.

4   Meanwhile, using a vegetable peeler or mandolin, peel the courgette, then the asparagus into long thin ribbons.

5   Cook the courgette on a heated lightly oiled chargrill pan (or in a frying pan) for 1 minute each side or until grill marks appear.

6   Place the asparagus and peas in a medium heatproof bowl, cover with boiling water; stand for 1 minute. Drain. Cool under running water; drain. Pat dry with paper towel.

7   Make the tahini yogurt. Combine the ingredients in a small bowl; season with salt and pepper to taste. Cover; refrigerate until needed.

8   Just before serving, fill the cooled tart case with the tahini yogurt. Top with courgette, asparagus, peas, and mint.

TIP

You can make the tart case and tahini yogurt several hours ahead. Assemble just before serving.

Classic sausage rolls

PREP + COOK TIME **40 MINUTES** | MAKES **12**

While there are endless recipes for sausage rolls, nothing beats a classic version. An easy way to make sure you get an equal amount of filling mixture in each sausage roll is to pipe it down the length of the pastry, using a piping bag fitted with a 2cm plain tube.

1 medium onion (150g), finely chopped

½ cup (35g) stale breadcrumbs (see tips)

500g sausage mince

500g minced beef

1 egg

1 tbsp tomato paste

1 tbsp barbecue sauce

2 tbsp finely chopped fresh flat-leaf parsley

6 sheets puff pastry

1 egg, lightly beaten, extra

2 tbsp sesame seeds

1 Preheat oven to 220°C (200°C fan/425°F/Gas 7). Line oven trays with baking paper.

2 Combine the onion, breadcrumbs, sausage mince and beef, egg, tomato paste, barbecue sauce, and parsley in a large bowl.

3 Cut the pastry sheets in half lengthways. Place equal amounts of the filling mixture lengthways along the centre of each pastry piece; roll each pastry piece, from one wide edge, to enclose the filling. Cut each roll into six pieces; place the rolls, seam-side down, on the oven trays. Brush with the extra egg, sprinkle with sesame seeds.

4 Bake the sausage rolls for 25 minutes or until golden and puffed. Serve the rolls hot with tomato sauce (ketchup) or chutney, if you like.

TIP

To make stale breadcrumbs, use 2–3 day old bread and process in batches.

Lentil sausage rolls

PREP + COOK TIME **45 MINUTES** | MAKES **8**

A filling of gently spiced lentils and roasted pistachios encased in light and crispy filo pastry reinvents the sausage roll. This wholesome nutritious version is completely meat free and is great for healthy snacking or a light lunch.

2 x 400g cans lentils, drained, rinsed

1 small onion (80g), finely grated

2 garlic cloves, crushed

1/3 cup (45g) chopped roasted pistachios

1 tsp sweet paprika

1 tsp ground cumin

1/4 tsp ground cinnamon

1/4 tsp dried chilli flakes

1 egg, lightly beaten

salt and freshly ground black pepper

10 sheets filo pastry

cooking-oil spray

1/4 tsp sumac

1 Preheat oven to 200°C (180°C fan/400°F/Gas 6). Line an oven tray with baking paper.

2 Place the lentils in a bowl; mash lightly. Add the remaining ingredients, except the filo pastry, oil spray, and sumac; stir to combine. Season with salt and pepper.

3 Layer five sheets of filo, spraying each sheet with oil. Place half the lentil mixture along one long side of the filo; roll to enclose the filling.

4 Cut into four even lengths. Place on the oven tray; spray with oil. Repeat with the remaining filo, oil, and lentil mixture to make 8 rolls in total.

5 Sprinkle the rolls with sumac; bake for 30 minutes or until golden. Serve the rolls as they are or with one of the sauces on pages on 144.

Lentil sausage roll variations

Make the lentil sausage rolls on page 143 but omit, swap, and add ingredients as directed in the individual recipes below to enjoy a different topping. Serve the sausage roll variation of your choice with either of the sauces below, if you like.

Lemon thyme salt sprinkle

Make the lentil sausage rolls, combining the sumac with 2 teaspoons of sea salt flakes, 2 teaspoons of finely grated lemon rind and 1 tablespoon of coarsely chopped fresh lemon thyme leaves in a small bowl. Sprinkle the mixture on the sausage rolls before baking as directed.

Mixed seed sprinkle

Make the lentil sausage rolls, omitting the sumac. Instead, combine 2 teaspoons of poppy seeds, 1 teaspoon of caraway seeds, 1 teaspoon of sesame seeds, 1 teaspoon of linseeds (flaxseeds) and 1 teaspoon of sea salt flakes in a small bowl. Sprinkle the mixture on the rolls before baking as directed.

Yogurt mustard sauce

Combine 1 cup (280g) Greek yogurt and 2 teaspoons of wholegrain mustard (or Dijon mustard) in a small bowl with 2 tablespoons of finely chopped fresh dill sprigs or mint leaves. Season with salt and freshly ground black pepper. Serve the lentil sausage rolls with the sauce.

Tomato sauce

Heat 1 tablespoon of oil in a saucepan; cook 1 medium (150g) finely chopped onion until soft. Stir in a 400g can diced tomatoes and 2 tablespoons each of brown sugar, tomato paste, and vinegar. Simmer for 20 minutes until thickened. Process until smooth. Serve the lentil sausage rolls with the sauce.

Rogan josh lamb pie

PREP + COOK TIME **3 HOURS + COOLING** | SERVES **6**

Rogan Josh, Persian in origin, is a Kashmiri dish and it's this aromatic lamb curry that forms the basis of this delicious golden pastry topped pie. Perfect for a cosy night in, this fragrant filling will take your pie to another level.

1kg diced lamb shoulder

$\frac{1}{3}$ cup (50g) plain flour

2 tbsp vegetable oil

2 medium onions (300g), thinly sliced

$\frac{1}{2}$ cup (135g) rogan josh curry paste

400g can chopped tomatoes

2 cups (500ml) salt-reduced beef stock

1 sheet puff pastry

2 tsp milk

$\frac{1}{4}$ tsp cumin seeds

1   Toss the lamb in the flour; shake away the excess. Heat the oil in a large saucepan; cook the lamb, in batches, until well browned. Remove from the pan.

2   Cook the onion in the same pan, stirring, until softened. Add the curry paste to the pan; cook, stirring, until fragrant. Return the lamb to the pan with the canned tomatoes and stock; bring to the boil. Reduce the heat; simmer, covered, for $1\frac{1}{2}$ hours. Remove the lid; simmer for 30 minutes or until tender. Season with salt and pepper to taste. Cool.

3   Preheat oven to 220°C (200°C fan/425°F/Gas 7).

4   Spoon the curry filling into a 24cm pie dish (1.5-litre/6-cup). Place the pastry over the filling; trim off the excess. Press around the edge with a fork to seal. Cut three slits in the centre of the pastry. Brush the pastry with milk; sprinkle with the cumin seeds. Place on an oven tray.

5   Bake the pie for 30 minutes or until browned.

Chunky beef and mushroom pies

PREP + COOK TIME **3 HOURS + REFRIGERATION** | MAKES **6**

Here tender chunks of beef and fresh mushrooms are brought together in a rich gravy for the ultimate comfort food. These classic pies make a great dinner on a cold night – serve with mashed potatoes and green vegetables, if you like.

600g beef chuck steak (braising steak)

2 tbsp plain flour

2 tbsp olive oil

1 small onion (80g), finely chopped

2 garlic cloves, crushed

125g mushrooms, sliced

400g can chopped tomatoes

³/₄ cup (180ml) beef stock

2 tbsp tomato paste

2 tbsp Worcestershire sauce

salt and freshly ground black pepper

3 sheets shortcrust pastry

3 sheets puff pastry

1 egg, lightly beaten

1   Preheat oven to 160°C (140°C fan/325°F/Gas 3).

2   Cut the beef into 4cm pieces. Coat the beef in the flour; shake off the excess. Heat half the oil in a large casserole dish over a medium-high heat; cook the beef, in batches, until browned. Remove from the dish.

3   Heat the remaining oil in the same dish over a medium heat; cook the onion, garlic, and mushrooms, stirring, until the vegetables soften. Return the beef to the dish with the tomatoes, stock, tomato paste, and Worcestershire sauce; bring to the boil. Place the lid on the dish, transfer to the oven; cook for 2 hours or until thickened slightly. Check the amount of liquid throughout cooking; you may need to add a little more stock. Season with salt and pepper. Cool.

4   Oil six 10cm x 13cm oval pie tins (²/₃ cup/ 160ml capacity). Using one upturned tin as a guide, cut six ovals from the shortcrust pastry. Ease the pastry into the tins, pressing into the bottoms and sides; trim edges. Place the tins on oven trays; refrigerate for 30 minutes.

5   Increase oven temperature to 200°C (180°C fan/400°F/Gas 6).

6   Line the pastry cases with baking paper; fill with dried beans or rice. Bake for 10 minutes. Carefully remove the paper and beans; bake for a further 5 minutes. Cool.

7   Cut six 16cm (6¹/₂in) ovals from the puff pastry. Fill the pastry cases with the beef filling; brush the edges with egg. Top the cases with the puff pastry ovals; press the edges with a fork to seal. Brush the tops with egg; cut steam holes in the tops.

8   Bake pies for 25 minutes or until lightly browned.

Sweet potato tarte tartin

PREP + COOK TIME **1 HOUR 40 MINUTES + REFRIGERATION** | SERVES **6**

This autumnal twist on the classic French dessert replaces apples with sweet potatoes for a savoury version. Light pastry is topped with sticky sweet caramelised onions and sweet potato, and finished with a crumbling of contrasting piquant goat's cheese.

20g butter

1 tbsp olive oil

1 tbsp pure maple syrup

3 garlic cloves, thinly sliced

1 tbsp fresh lemon thyme leaves, plus extra to serve

350g sweet potato, cut into 1cm slices

salt and freshly ground black pepper

1 cup (250ml) water

1 egg yolk

1 tbsp milk or water

2 sheets frozen puff pastry, thawed slightly

100g soft goat's cheese

caramelised onions

20g butter

1 tbsp olive oil

4 medium onions (800g), finely sliced

¼ cup (60ml) balsamic vinegar

2 tbsp pure maple syrup

1 tbsp Dijon mustard

1 Make the caramelised onions. Heat the butter and olive oil in a large heavy-based frying pan over a medium heat; cook the onion, stirring frequently, for 20 minutes or until very soft and golden. Add the vinegar, maple syrup, and mustard; cook for a further 20 minutes over a low heat or until caramelised and the mixture has reduced. Season with salt and pepper.

2 Heat the butter, olive oil, and maple syrup in a 30cm ovenproof frying pan over a medium heat. Add the garlic; cook, stirring, for 1 minute. Remove the pan from the heat. Sprinkle the thyme over the bottom of the pan; pack the sweet potato slices, in a single layer, on top; season with salt and pepper. Pour half the water over the sweet potato. Return the pan to the heat; cook for 8 minutes or until the water evaporates. Add the remaining water; cook for a further 8 minutes or until the sweet potato slices are browned underneath. Remove the pan from the heat; cool for 5 minutes.

3 Spoon the caramelised onion evenly over the sweet potato layer using the back of a spoon. Refrigerate until the mixture has cooled completely.

4 Preheat oven to 200°C (180°C fan/400°F/Gas 6).

5 Whisk the egg yolk and milk together. Cut each pasty sheet on a diagonal into two triangles. Make one larger square from the four triangles; use a little egg mixture to join the pastry together. Place the pastry square over the tart; trim the excess. Fold, nip, and tuck the pastry edges around the tart filling. Brush the pastry with a little more egg mixture; prick lightly with a fork.

6 Bake the tart for 20 minutes or until golden. Leave in the pan for 5 minutes.

7 To serve, place the pan over a medium heat for 30 seconds to loosen the base mixture; quickly turn the tart onto a wooden board or plate. Top with the crumbled goat's cheese and extra thyme.

Lamb and mushroom pies

PREP + COOK TIME **50 MINUTES + COOLING** | SERVES **4**

These individual lamb pies are so simple to make and are great for a staple weeknight dinner. Juicy lamb is encased in golden pastry and baked to perfection. Serve with mushy peas and tomato sauce (ketchup), if you like.

2 sheets frozen shortcrust pastry, just thawed

2 tbsp olive oil

300g coarsely chopped mushrooms

500g minced lamb

1 cup (250g) bottled tomato and basil pasta sauce

salt and freshly ground black pepper

1 egg, lightly beaten

1 Preheat oven to 180°C (160°C fan/350°F/Gas 4).

2 Cut one pastry sheet into four squares. Line four oiled 9.5cm (base measurement) pie tins with pastry squares; trim the excess pastry.

3 Heat the olive oil in a large frying pan over a medium-high heat; cook the mushrooms, stirring occasionally, for 5 minutes or until golden. Add the lamb; cook, stirring to break up the lumps, for 5 minutes or until browned. Stir in the tomato sauce; season with salt and pepper to taste. Cool for 10 minutes.

4 Fill the pastry cases with the lamb mixture. Brush the pastry edges with egg. Cut four rounds large enough to cover the pie tops, from the remaining pastry sheet; cover the filling with the pastry rounds, pressing the edges together with a fork to seal. Brush the pastry with the egg; make small cuts in the top of each pie.

5 Bake the pies for 25 minutes or until browned. Carefully, take the pies out of the tins; place the pies on an oven tray, cover loosely with foil. Bake the pies, on the bottom shelf of the oven, for 5 minutes or until the pastry bases are cooked through.

BREADS, SCONES, AND SCROLLS

Fill your kitchen with the delightful aroma of freshly baked goods, from sweet and sticky buns through to fluffy scones, savoury scrolls, crusty loaves, and golden rolls.

Chelsea buns

PREP + COOK TIME **1 HOUR 30 MINUTES + STANDING** | MAKES **12**

These delicious sticky, buttery buns were created in the 18th century in the Chelsea area
of London by the Chelsea Bun House, apparently a favourite haunt of the British royal family.
Our version is sprinkled with chopped roasted pecans and glazed with honey.

4 tsp (14g) dry yeast

1¹/₂ tbsp caster sugar

1¹/₂ cups (375ml) warm milk

3 cups (560g) plain flour

1¹/₂ tsp ground cinnamon

2 tsp finely grated orange rind

1 egg, lightly beaten

60g butter, melted

2 tbsp raspberry jam

¹/₄ cup (55g) firmly packed brown sugar

¹/₂ cup (60g) chopped roasted pecans

3 tsp warmed honey

1 Combine the yeast, 1 teaspoon of the caster sugar, and the warm milk in a large bowl. Cover; stand in a warm place for 10 minutes or until frothy.

2 Add the sifted flour and the remaining caster sugar to the yeast mixture in a bowl with the cinnamon, orange rind, egg, and two-thirds of the butter; mix to a soft dough. Knead the dough on a floured surface for 10 minutes or until smooth and elastic. Place the dough in a large greased bowl. Cover; stand in a warm place for 1 hour or until doubled in size.

3 Grease two deep 22cm round cake pans. Roll the dough on a floured surface into a 23cm x 36cm rectangle; brush with the remaining butter, then spread with jam. Sprinkle with brown sugar and pecans, leaving a 2cm border. Roll the dough up firmly from one long side like a swiss roll. Cut into 12 pieces; place six pieces, cut-side up, in each pan. Cover; stand in a warm place for 30 minutes or until it has risen slightly.

4 Preheat oven to 200°C (180°C fan/400°F/Gas 6).

5 Bake the buns for 40 minutes or until golden brown. Turn the buns, top-side up, onto a wire rack; brush with honey.

Dark chocolate cherry and walnut soda bread

PREP + COOK TIME **1 HOUR 30 MINUTES** | MAKES **1 LOAF** SERVES **8**

This super-easy bread relies on the reaction between alkaline bicarbonate of soda and acidic buttermilk, to produce carbon dioxide for aeration. Since the reaction is immediate upon mixing, make sure you get baking quick smart.

4 cups (600g) plain flour

$^1/_4$ cup (55g) caster sugar

2 tsp bicarbonate of soda

1 tsp sea salt

1$^1/_2$ tsp ground cardamom

100g cold unsalted butter, chopped

1$^3/_4$ cups (430ml) buttermilk

1 egg, lightly beaten

100g dark chocolate, chopped

$^3/_4$ cup (75g) roasted walnuts, chopped

$^3/_4$ cup (115g) dried cherries or cranberries

1 egg white

2 tbsp caster sugar, extra

2 tsp icing sugar

1   Preheat oven to 180°C (160°C fan/350°F/Gas 4). Line an oven tray with baking paper.

2   Sift the flour, sugar, bicarbonate of soda, salt, and cardamom into a large bowl. Rub in the butter with your fingertips until the mixture resembles coarse crumbs. Make a well in the centre.

3   Whisk the buttermilk and egg in a medium bowl; pour into the well. Using a knife, cut the liquid through the flour mixture until it starts to clump. Add the chocolate, walnuts, and cherries. Turn the dough onto a lightly floured surface; knead gently until the dough just comes together. Shape into a 16cm round. Place on the lined tray.

4   Lightly beat the egg white and the extra sugar in a small bowl with a fork. Brush the mixture over the top of the loaf.

5   Bake the loaf for 1 hour or until golden and the bread sounds hollow when tapped. Serve warm or at room temperature, dusted with icing sugar.

TIPS

- Serve sliced bread fresh or toasted with ricotta and honey.
- Try other dried fruit and nuts, such as sultanas and pecans.

Banana bread

PREP + COOK TIME **1 HOUR 15 MINUTES** | SERVES **8**

This moist banana bread tastes wonderful straight from the oven and is best served in thick slices. If you're eating it a day or two after baking, try toasting it and serving with lashings of butter.

125g butter, softened

1 cup (220g) firmly packed brown sugar

1 tsp vanilla extract

2 eggs

1½ cups (400g) mashed ripe banana

¼ cup (60ml) maple syrup

1⅔ cups (250g) plain flour

1 tsp baking powder

1 tsp bicarbonate of soda

1 tsp ground cinnamon

¼ tsp salt flakes

½ cup (25g) coarsely chopped roasted walnuts

1 Preheat oven to 160°C (140°C fan/325°F/Gas 3).

2 Grease a 13cm x 26cm, 8-cup (2-litre) loaf pan; line with baking paper.

3 Beat the butter, sugar, and vanilla extract in a medium bowl with an electric mixer until paler and fluffy. Beat in the eggs, one at a time, until just combined, then the mashed banana and maple syrup. Sift over the flour, baking powder, bicarbonate of soda, cinnamon, and salt.

4 Add the walnuts; stir with a large spoon until combined. Spoon into the pan; smooth the surface.

5 Bake for 1 hour or until a skewer inserted into the centre comes out clean. Leave in the pan for 10 minutes before turning, top-side up, onto a wire rack to cool.

Banana bread variations

Banana bread can easily be adapted to accommodate your favourite flavour combinations. Make the plain version on page 161 omitting, swapping, and adding ingredients as directed in the individual recipes below.

Chocolate coconut banana bread

Make the banana bread recipe, omitting the ground cinnamon and using ¹/₂ cup (95g) dark or milk chocolate chips instead of walnuts, and adding ¹/₄ cup (10g) coconut flakes. Spoon the mixture into the pan; smooth the surface. Scatter the top with an extra 2 tablespoons each of dark or milk chocolate chips and coconut chips. Continue as directed in the recipe.

Peanut butter and raspberry banana bread

Make the banana bread recipe, using ¹/₄ cup (60ml) vegetable oil instead of the butter, and ¹/₂ cup (140g) smooth peanut butter along with ³/₄ cup (95g) fresh raspberries instead of the walnuts. Spoon the mixture into the lined pan; smooth the surface. Sprinkle the top with 1 tablespoon of demerara sugar. Continue as directed in the recipe.

Hummingbird banana bread

Drain 440g canned crushed pineapple; discard the juice. Make the banana bread recipe, using ¹/₂ cup (125ml) vegetable oil instead of butter and adding the drained pineapple along with the banana. Continue as directed. Beat 125g softened cream cheese and 1¹/₂ cups (240g) sifted icing sugar with an electric mixer until light and fluffy. Spread the frosting on the cooled loaf, dust with extra cinnamon.

Cream cheese filled banana bread

Beat 125g softened cream cheese, ¹/₄ cup (55g) caster sugar, 1 egg, 1 teaspoon of finely grated lemon rind, and 2 tablespoons of plain flour with an electric mixer until smooth. Make the banana bread recipe; spread half the mixture in the pan, smooth the surface. Top with the filling, spreading to the edge. Spread evenly with the remaining bread mixture. Bake as directed.

Spinach and three cheese muffins

PREP + COOK TIME **45 MINUTES** | MAKES **12**

These light and fluffy vegetarian cheese muffins are great for snacking or serving as finger food at a lunch party. They are delicious enjoyed warm straight from the oven, but also make a wonderful lunchbox addition.

2 tbsp olive oil

1 small onion (80g), finely chopped

100g baby spinach leaves

2 cups (300g) self-raising flour

80g butter, melted

1 egg

1 cup (250ml) buttermilk

1/2 cup (50g) coarsely grated mozzarella

1/2 cup (40g) coarsely grated parmesan

100g blue cheese, crumbled

1 Preheat oven to 200°C (180°C fan/400°F/Gas 6). Grease a 12-hole (1/3 cup/80ml) muffin pan.

2 Heat the olive oil in a medium frying pan; cook the onion, stirring for 5 minutes or until the onion softens. Add the spinach; cook, stirring, for 1 minute or until wilted. Cool.

3 Sift the flour into a large bowl; stir in the combined butter, egg, and buttermilk. Add the cheeses and the spinach mixture to the flour mixture; mix gently to combine. Do not over-mix; the mixture should be lumpy. Spoon the mixture into the pan holes.

4 Bake the muffins for 20 minutes or until a skewer inserted into the centre comes out clean. Leave in the pan for 5 minutes before turning, top-side up, onto a wire rack. Serve warm.

Pizza scrolls

PREP + COOK TIME **40 MINUTES** | MAKES **9**

These easy-to-make pizza scrolls are delicious eaten warm or cold and are a fun alternative for kids' lunchboxes. For a meat-free version, try using thinly sliced mushrooms instead of the pepperoni.

2 cups (300g) self-raising flour

1/2 tsp bicarbonate of soda

1 tsp salt

50g cold butter, coarsely chopped

3/4 cup (180ml) buttermilk, approximately

2 tbsp store-bought pizza sauce

2 tbsp barbecue sauce

1/2 small red onion (50g), thinly sliced

1/2 small green capsicum (pepper) (75g), thinly sliced

100g sliced pepperoni, coarsely chopped

1/2 cup (100g) canned pineapple pieces, drained well, coarsely chopped (see tip)

1/3 cup (55g) drained sliced kalamata olives

1 cup (120g) mozzarella

1 Preheat oven to 200°C (180°C fan/400°F/Gas 6). Oil a 22cm square cake pan.

2 Sift the flour, bicarbonate of soda, and salt into a medium bowl; rub in the butter with your fingertips. Add enough buttermilk to mix to a soft, sticky dough. Turn the dough onto a floured surface; knead lightly until smooth. Roll the dough into a 30cm x 40cm rectangle.

3 Spread the dough with the combined sauces; sprinkle with the onion, capsicum, pepperoni, pineapple, olives, and half the mozzarella. Roll the dough tightly from the long side. Using a serrated knife, trim the ends. Cut the roll into 9 slices; place the scrolls, cut-side up, in the pan. Sprinkle the scrolls with the remaining mozzarella.

4 Bake the scrolls for 25 minutes or until cooked through.

TIP

The pineapple must be drained well, otherwise it will make the scrolls soggy. Once the pineapple pieces have been drained from the can, pat them dry with paper towel.

Pumpkin and parmesan scones

PREP + COOK TIME **30 MINUTES** | MAKES **10**

To ensure these scrumptious savoury scones rise evenly with straight sides, cut out the scones using a sharp metal cutter; remove the cutter in an upward, rather than a twisting motion. Scones are best made close to serving time.

60g butter, softened

1 tbsp wholegrain mustard

1/2 cup (40g) finely grated parmesan

1 egg yolk

1 cup (250g) cooked, cold mashed butternut pumpkin (butternut squash) (see tips)

2 1/2 cups (355g) self-raising flour

1/2 tsp salt

1/4 tsp bicarbonate of soda

2 tbsp milk

1 Preheat oven to 200°C (180°C fan/400°F/Gas 6). Grease and line an oven tray with baking paper.

2 Stir the butter, mustard, parmesan, and egg yolk in a large bowl until combined. Stir in the mashed pumpkin. Sift the self-raising flour, salt, and bicarbonate of soda over the pumpkin mixture. Using a flat-bladed knife, cut the flour mixture through the pumpkin mixture to make a soft dough.

3 Turn the dough onto a floured surface and knead lightly. Roll or pat the dough out to approximately 2cm thick. Cut out the scones using a 6cm floured cutter. Place on the oven tray; brush the tops with a little of the milk.

4 Bake the scones for 14 minutes or until golden and hollow sounding when tapped. Transfer, top-side up, to a wire rack to cool. Serve with butter, if you like.

TIPS

- You will need to cook 300g butternut pumpkin (butternut squash) for this recipe.
- The trick to beautiful light scones is to handle the mixture as little as possible.

Seeded flatbreads

PREP + COOK TIME 1 HOUR + REFRIGERATION | MAKES 3

These crisp flatbreads are perfect for dipping or topping and their seed content makes them super nutritious. Linseeds and chia seeds are rich in dietary fibre, loaded with nutrients, and high in Omega-3 fats.

³/₄ cup (110g) white spelt flour

1 tsp baking powder

2 tbsp linseeds (flaxseeds)

2 tbsp black chia seeds

salt and freshly ground black pepper

¹/₂ cup (140g) Greek yogurt

1 tsp salt flakes

1 Preheat oven to 200°C (180°C fan/400°F/Gas 6). Grease three large oven trays.

2 Sift the flour and baking powder into a bowl; stir in the linseeds and chia seeds. Season with salt and pepper. Add the yogurt; stir with a butter knife to combine.

3 Knead the dough in the bowl. Divide the dough into three portions; roll out each portion on a floured piece of baking paper into a 12cm x 42cm rectangle. Carefully lift the dough on the paper onto the oven trays.

4 Bake for 15 minutes or until golden and crisp. Scatter with salt.

Seeded flatbreads variations

Choose your favourite flavour combinations to take your flatbreads to another level. Make the seeded flatbreads on page 171 and then try one of the following toppings to transform them into a delicious lunch.

Red onion, pear, and goat's cheese

Heat 2 tablespoons of olive oil in a frying pan over high heat; cook 1/4 cup (6g) sage leaves for 30 seconds until crisp. Remove with a slotted spoon; drain. In the same pan, cook 2 medium red onions (340g) and 2 pears (460g). Cut into wedges with 1 crushed garlic clove; stir for 7 minutes until soft. Spoon onto the seeded flatbread, top with 100g crumbled goat's cheese and crispy sage.

Smashed avocado and feta

Place 3 chopped avocados (750g) in a bowl with 1 crushed garlic clove, 1 seeded, finely chopped long red chilli, 1 teaspoon of ground cumin, 2 tablespoons of lime juice, and 1/4 cup (8g) chopped fresh coriander; mash with a fork. Spread the mixture on the seeded flatbread; top with 100g crumbled feta and extra coriander leaves, if you like.

Prosciutto and melon

Spread the warm seeded flatbread with 150g garlic and herb flavoured cream cheese. Divide 12 slices (180g) prosciutto (or shaved ham) among the breads with 250g thinly sliced melon. Season with freshly ground black pepper and drizzle with a little extra virgin olive oil.

Tomato and mozzarella

Serve the seeded flatbread topped with 6 small (360g) sliced tomatoes, 200g roughly torn buffalo mozzarella, 40g wild rocket leaves, and 2 tablespoons of pine nuts. Season with salt and freshly ground black pepper; drizzle with a little extra virgin olive oil.

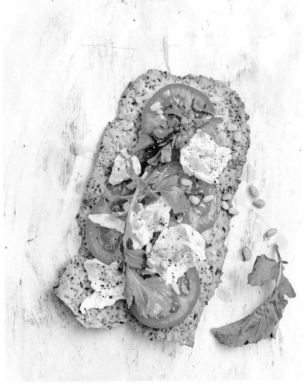

Rosemary and garlic focaccia

PREP + COOK TIME **1 HOUR 15 MINUTES + STANDING AND COOLING** | SERVES **8**

Perfectly crisp on the outside, soft and chewy on the inside, this fragrant focaccia is studded with rosemary and roasted garlic. Serve with soups, pasta dishes, or salads. If you like, omit the poached garlic and use black or green olives instead.

15 garlic cloves, peeled

1 cup (250ml) extra virgin olive oil

2²/₃ cups (400g) plain flour

2 tsp sea salt flakes

1 tsp caster sugar

1 tsp (4g) dried yeast

1¹/₄ cups (310ml) warm water, approximately

2 tbsp fresh rosemary sprigs

1 Place the garlic and olive oil in a small saucepan over a low heat, making sure the garlic is completely covered by the oil. Bring to a gentle simmer; cook for 20 minutes or until soft (but not mushy). Using a slotted spoon, remove the garlic from the oil; cut any large cloves in half. Reserve the oil (see tips); cool.

2 Place the flour, 1 teaspoon of crumbled sea salt flakes, the sugar, and the yeast in a large bowl of an electric mixer fitted with a dough hook. Mix on medium speed until just combined. Add the water and 2 tablespoons of the reserved oil; mix until well combined. Mix on medium speed for 15 minutes.

3 Transfer the dough to an oiled large bowl; lightly oil the top of the dough. Cover the bowl with plastic wrap (cling film). Stand at room temperature for 3 hours or until the dough has doubled in size.

4 Line a 30cm x 40cm oven tray with baking paper; brush the paper with 1 tablespoon of the reserved oil. Using oiled hands, press and spread the dough on the tray; don't stretch the dough too much. Rest the dough for 10 minutes. Repeat stretching the dough with your fingertips to fit the tray. Stand in a warm place for 1 hour. Poke dimples into the dough with your fingertips; press the poached garlic into the dimples, sprinkle with the rosemary.

5 Meanwhile, preheat oven to 200°C (180°C fan/400°F/Gas 6).

6 Drizzle the dough with 2 tablespoons of the reserved oil; sprinkle with the remaining salt flakes. Bake the focaccia for 25 minutes or until golden and it sounds hollow when tapped on the base. Serve warm.

TIPS

- Keep any leftover reserved oil from the poached garlic to use in stir-fries or for marinating and grilling meat, fish, and chicken.
- Focaccia is best made on the day of serving. It can be frozen for up to 2 months.

No-knead spelt and linseed bread

PREP + COOK TIME **50 MINUTES + STANDING** | MAKES **1 LOAF**

Spelt is an ancient grain with similarities to wheat; while it is not gluten-free, some people find it easier to digest. Unlike plain flour, which is refined by removing the germ and bran, the nutritious part of the spelt grain remains when it is milled into flour.

2 tsp (7g) dried yeast

1^1/$_3$ cups (330ml) lukewarm water

1^1/$_3$ cups (200g) wholemeal spelt flour

^{1}/$_3$ cup (60g) linseeds (flaxseeds)

2 tsp cumin seeds

1 tbsp olive oil

2 tsp golden syrup

2 tsp sea salt

2 cups (300g) bread flour

1 tsp bread flour, extra

1 tsp cumin seeds, extra

1 Place the yeast and water in a large bowl; whisk until combined. Add the spelt flour, seeds, olive oil, and golden syrup; stir until combined.

2 Add the salt and bread flour; mix into a sticky dough. Cover the bowl with plastic wrap (cling film); stand in a warm place for 1 hour or until the dough has doubled in size.

3 Turn the dough out onto a lightly floured work surface; press out to form a 25cm round. Fold the dough under itself to form a 16cm round loaf. Place the dough seam-side down on a baking-paper-lined oven tray. Dust with extra bread flour; cover with a clean tea towel. Stand in a warm place for 45 minutes or until almost doubled in size.

4 Preheat oven to 220°C (200°C fan/425°F/Gas 7).

5 Using a small sharp knife or razor blade, cut five slashes across the top of the bread. Sprinkle with extra cumin seeds.

6 Bake the bread for 30 minutes or until browned and the bread sounds hollow when tapped.

TIP

This bread is great for sandwiches or served alongside soups.

Courgette and corn loaf

PREP + COOK TIME **2 HOURS 15 MINUTES** | SERVES **12**

This is a simple stir and bake recipe, with no kneading or resting period required. It results in a deliciously savoury golden loaf perfect smeared with butter or topped with cheese. You will need to use traditional polenta for this recipe, not the instant variety.

1 medium courgette (120g)

2 cups (300g) self-raising flour

1 tsp salt

1 cup (170g) polenta

3/4 cup (90g) coarsely grated cheddar

1 fresh long red chilli, seeded, finely chopped

420g canned corn kernels (sweetcorn), drained, rinsed

310g canned creamed corn

1/2 cup (125ml) buttermilk

3 eggs

40g butter, melted

1 Preheat oven to 180°C (160°C fan/350°F/Gas 4). Oil a 14cm x 23cm loaf pan; line the bottom and sides with baking paper.

2 Coarsely grate the courgette, place in a sieve; squeeze out any excess water, drain well.

3 Sift the flour and salt into a large bowl; stir in the polenta, 1/2 cup (60g) of the cheddar, and the chilli. Stir in the combined courgette, corn kernels, creamed corn, buttermilk, eggs, and butter. Spread the mixture into the pan; sprinkle with the remaining cheddar.

4 Bake the loaf for 2 hours (cover the pan with foil if it starts to overbrown). Leave in the pan for 5 minutes before turning, top-side up, onto a wire rack to cool.

TIP

Removing the seeds and membrane from the chilli lessens the heat; keep the seeds, if you prefer.

Beer bread

PREP + COOK TIME **45 MINUTES + STANDING AND COOLING** | SERVES **8**

Serve this bread with ham hock or corned beef, or chunks of vintage cheddar and pickle with a few crisp salad leaves for a memorable sandwich. Or serve chunks of bread with slow-cooked meat dishes or topped with cheese and grilled to accompany a French onion soup.

1 tsp (4g) dried yeast

1 tbsp malt extract

$2^3/_4$ cups (410g) bread flour

1 cup (250ml) dark ale, at room temperature

2 tsp sea salt flakes

2 tbsp bread flour, extra

1 Place the yeast, malt extract, and flour in a large bowl of an electric mixer fitted with a dough hook. On low speed, gradually add the ale, mixing until just combined. Add the salt; mix until combined and the dough forms a soft ball.

2 Transfer the dough to an oiled large bowl; cover with plastic wrap (cling film). Stand in a warm place for $1^1/_2$ hours or until the dough has doubled in size.

3 Oil an oven tray. Knead the dough on a lightly floured surface until smooth. Shape the dough into a 10cm x 25cm loaf. Place on the tray; cover with oiled plastic wrap (cling film). Stand in a warm place for 1 hour or until the dough has doubled in size.

4 Meanwhile, preheat oven to 230°C (210°C fan/450°F/Gas 8).

5 Sprinkle the dough with extra flour. Using a sharp knife, cut one long slash down the centre of the loaf.

6 Bake the loaf for 15 minutes. Reduce oven temperature to 200°C (180°C fan/400°F/Gas 6); bake for a further 15 minutes or until golden and the base sounds hollow when tapped. Transfer to a wire rack to cool.

TIPS

- Malt extract is a thick dark syrup available from large supermarkets.
- This bread is best made on the day of serving, though can be frozen for up to 2 months.

Quinoa and seed cheese quick loaf

PREP + COOK TIME **1 HOUR 5 MINUTES + STANDING** | MAKES **12 SLICES**

This crusty loaf can be made dairy-free by following the non-dairy alternatives in the ingredients list. It is delicious served with soups or stews, or on its own with butter and golden syrup, rich jam, or creamy cheeses.

¼ cup (50g) red quinoa

½ cup (125ml) boiling water

3 cups (450g) self-raising flour

2 tsp sea salt

40g butter or firm coconut oil, chopped

¼ cup (50g) roasted buckwheat

2 tbsp linseeds (flaxseeds)

2 tbsp pepitas (pumpkin seeds)

¾ cup (90g) grated vintage cheddar or soy cheese

½ cup (125ml) milk or almond milk

¾ cup (180ml) water, approximately

1 Place the quinoa and boiling water in a small heatproof bowl. Stand for 20 minutes. Drain well.

2 Preheat oven to 180°C (160°C fan/350°F/Gas 4). Flour a large oven tray.

3 Place the flour and salt in a large bowl; rub in the butter with your fingertips. Stir in the soaked quinoa, buckwheat, linseeds, pepitas, and cheddar. Stir in the milk and enough of the water to mix to a soft dough. Knead the dough on a floured surface until smooth.

4 Place the dough on the floured tray; press into a 16cm round. Brush with a little extra water or milk. Cut a 1cm deep cross in the top of the dough.

5 Bake for 50 minutes, turning the tray halfway through cooking time, or until browned and it sounds hollow when tapped on the base.

TIP

Quinoa is available in red, white, and black; all are nutritionally equal, however red quinoa has a slightly higher fibrous texture so holds its shape better after cooking.

Olive and feta rolls

PREP + COOK TIME **1 HOUR 10 MINUTES + STANDING** | MAKES **8**

Bring a taste of the Mediterranean to your baking with these lovely little golden rolls that are bursting with sunshine flavours. Delicious served with soups and salads, or they make a perfect side to be enjoyed with grilled meat dishes.

2 tsp (7g) dried yeast

2 tsp honey

²/₃ cup (160ml) lukewarm water

2¹/₂ cups (375g) bread flour or plain flour

¹/₂ cup (85g) polenta

2 tsp dried oregano

1 tsp fine sea salt

¹/₃ cup (80ml) extra virgin olive oil

¹/₂ cup (125ml) lukewarm water, extra

1¹/₂ tbsp polenta, extra

²/₃ cup (80g) pitted black olives, halved

80g feta, crumbled coarsely

1 Combine the yeast, honey, and water in a small bowl; stir until the yeast dissolves. Cover; stand in a warm place for 10 minutes or until the mixture is frothy.

2 Combine the flour, polenta, oregano, and salt in a large bowl. Stir in the olive oil, yeast mixture, and the extra water until the mixture forms a soft dough. Knead the dough on a floured surface for 10 minutes or until smooth and elastic. (Or mix in an electric mixer fitted with a dough hook for 5 minutes or until smooth and elastic.)

3 Place the dough in a large oiled bowl; cover with plastic wrap (cling film). Stand in a warm place for 1 hour or until the dough has doubled in size.

4 Sprinkle a large oven tray with 2 teaspoons of the extra polenta. Turn the dough onto a lightly floured surface; gently knead in the olives and feta. Divide the dough into eight portions; shape each portion into a ball. Place the rolls on the tray, about 5cm apart. Brush the rolls with a little extra water; sprinkle with the remaining extra polenta. Cover the tray with a clean tea towel; stand in a warm place for 30 minutes or until the dough has almost doubled in size.

5 Meanwhile, preheat oven to 200°C (180°C fan/400°F/Gas 6).

6 Bake the rolls for 25 minutes or until golden. Transfer to a wire rack to cool slightly.

TIP

These rolls are best made on the day of serving, though they can also be frozen for up to 2 months.

Spiced pumpkin snacking loaf

PREP + COOK TIME **1 HOUR 20 MINUTES + COOLING** | SERVES **8**

A warmly fragranced, wonderfully moist, lightly spiced loaf perfect for autumn days. Serve in generous thick slices for snacking. This bread tastes even better when you let it sit for a day or so; store it in an airtight container.

2 cups (300g) self-raising flour

1 tsp sea salt flakes

1 tsp ground cumin

1 tsp ground coriander

1 tsp ground turmeric

1 tsp chilli flakes

1 cup (250g) mashed cooked butternut pumpkin (butternut squash) (see tip)

1/2 cup (125ml) buttermilk

60g butter, melted

2 eggs

1/4 cup (50g) pepitas (pumpkin seeds), coarsely chopped

1/4 cup (20g) finely grated parmesan

2 tsp fresh thyme leaves

1 Preheat oven to 180°C (160°C fan/350°F/Gas 4). Oil an 11cm x 18cm loaf pan; line the bottom with baking paper.

2 Combine the flour, salt, and spices in a large bowl; make a well in the centre. Stir in the combined mashed pumpkin, buttermilk, butter, and eggs until just combined. Spoon the mixture into the pan; smooth the surface. Sprinkle with the combined pepitas, parmesan, and thyme.

3 Bake the bread for 55 minutes. Leave in the pan for 10 minutes, before turning, top-side up, onto a wire rack. Cool for at least 30 minutes before serving.

TIP

You need to cook 400g butternut pumpkin (butternut squash) for the amount of mashed pumpkin in this recipe.

Conversion chart

A note on Australian measures

- One Australian metric measuring cup holds approximately 250ml.

- One Australian metric tablespoon holds 20ml.

- One Australian metric teaspoon holds 5ml.

- The difference between one country's measuring cups and another's is within a two- or three-teaspoon variance, and should not affect your cooking results.

- North America, New Zealand, and the United Kingdom use a 15ml tablespoon.

Using measures in this book

- All cup and spoon measurements are level.

- The most accurate way of measuring dry ingredients is to weigh them.

- When measuring liquids, use a clear glass or plastic jug with metric markings.

- We use large eggs with an average weight of 60g.

Dry measures

metric	imperial
15g	$1/2$oz
30g	1oz
60g	2oz
90g	3oz
125g	4oz ($1/4$lb)
155g	5oz
185g	6oz
220g	7oz
250g	8oz ($1/2$lb)
280g	9oz
315g	10oz
345g	11oz
375g	12oz ($3/4$lb)
410g	13oz
440g	14oz
470g	15oz
500g	16oz (1lb)
750g	24oz ($1\,1/2$lb)
1kg	32oz (2lb)

Liquid measures

metric	imperial
30ml	1 fluid oz
60ml	2 fluid oz
100ml	3 fluid oz
125ml	4 fluid oz
150ml	5 fluid oz
190ml	6 fluid oz
250ml	8 fluid oz
300ml	10 fluid oz
500ml	16 fluid oz
600ml	20 fluid oz
1000ml (1 litre)	$1\,3/4$ pints

Length measures

metric	imperial
3mm	$1/8$in
6mm	$1/4$in
1cm	$1/2$in
2cm	$3/4$in
2.5cm	1in
5cm	2in
6cm	$2\,1/2$in
8cm	3in
10cm	4in
13cm	5in
15cm	6in
18cm	7in
20cm	8in
22cm	9in
25cm	10in
28cm	11in
30cm	12in (1ft)

Oven temperatures

The oven temperatures in this book are for conventional ovens; if you have a fan-forced oven, decrease the temperature by 10–20 degrees.

	°C (Celsius)	°F (Fahrenheit)
Very slow	120	250
Slow	150	300
Moderately slow	160	325
Moderate	180	350
Moderately hot	200	400
Hot	220	425
Very hot	240	475

Index

A

almonds
  chocolate truffle almond slice 38
  frangipane 97
  nectarine and almond tart 97
Anzac biscuits 43
apples
  apple and brie tart 114
  apple ginger cakes with lemon icing 58
  pork and apple sausage rolls 118a
asparagus
  smoked salmon and asparagus quiche 124
avocado, smashed and feta flatbread 172

B

baked chocolate caramel cheesecake 85
banana bread 161
  chocolate coconut 162
  cream cheese filled 162
  hummingbird 162
  peanut butter and raspberry 162
beef
  beef and pea triangles 131
  chunky beef and mushroom pies 149
  classic sausage rolls 141
beer bread 180
beetroot and hazelnut tart, freeform 112
berries
  berry jam and vanilla palmiers 28
  blackberry swirl lemonade cupcakes 50
  blackberry swirl frosting 50
  peach and raspberry tarts 102
  peanut butter and raspberry banana bread 162
  raspberry and passionfruit mile-high layer cake 82
  raspberry and white chocolate friands 56
  raspberry coconut slice 24
biscotti, Florentine 30
biscuits and cookies

Anzac biscuits 43
caramel ginger crunchies 17
chocolate chip cookies 10
Florentine biscotti 30
gingerbread wreaths 32
hazelnut and dark choc cookies 12
honey jumbles 22
lemon and pistachios biscuits 36
M&M's biscuits 36
melting moments 18
oats and sultanas chocolate chip cookies 12
orange and poppyseed biscuits 36
peanut butter cup cookies 12
pecan and cinnamon biscuits 36
rich chocolate chip cookies 12
slice-and-bake biscuits 35
triple chocolate chip cookies 12
blackberries
  blackberry swirl lemonade cupcakes 50
  blackberry swirl frosting 50
blue cheese quiche 124
bread
  banana bread 161
  beer bread 180
  courgette and corn loaf 179
  dark chocolate cherry and walnut soda bread 158
  no-knead spelt and linseed bread 177
  olive and feta rolls 185
  quinoa and seed cheese quick loaf 182
  rosemary and garlic focaccia 174
  spiced pumpkin snacking loaf 186
brownies, 5-ingredient triple chocolate 14
buns, Chelsea 156
butter cake, classic 63

C

cakes see also cupcakes
  carrot 69
  cheesecake, New York 48
  chocolate slab 66
  classic butter 63
  coffee and walnut 53

devil's food 79
featherlight sponge 60
flourless chocolate 87
honey and fig tiramisu 88
lamingtons 80
New York cheesecake 48
one-bowl chocolate velvet 46
passionfruit and lemon syrup 90
raspberry and passionfruit mile-high layer 82
capsicum and goat's cheese quiche 124
caramel
  baked chocolate caramel cheesecake 85
  caramel éclairs 72
  caramel ginger crunchies 17
  chocolate caramel slice 21
  sauce 75
caramelised onions 151
carrot cake 69
cheese
  apple and brie tart 114
  blue cheese quiche 124
  capsicum and goat's cheese quiche 124
  olive and feta rolls 185
  pumpkin and parmesan scones 168
  quinoa and seed cheese quick loaf 182
  ricotta ginger frosting 70
  silver beet and cheese snails 134
  spinach and three cheese muffins 165
  tomato and goat's cheese tart with rice and seed crust 120
cheesecake
  baked chocolate caramel 85
  New York 48
Chelsea buns 156
chicken
  butter chicken hand pies 129
  chicken and leek pie 132
chocolate see also white chocolate
  5-ingredient triple chocolate brownies 14
  baked chocolate caramel cheesecake 85
  chocolate and hazelnut friands 56
  chocolate buttercream 66

chocolate caramel slice 21
chocolate chip cookies 10
chocolate coconut banana bread 162
chocolate glaze 46
chocolate slab cake 66
chocolate truffle almond slice 38
dark chocolate cherry and walnut soda bread 158
flourless chocolate cake 87
hazelnut and dark choc cookies 12
oats and sultanas chocolate chip cookies 12
one-bowl chocolate velvet cake 46
rich chocolate chip cookies 12
rich chocolate frosting 79
triple chocolate chip cookies 12
whipped milk choc peanut frosting 76
chunky beef and mushroom pies 149
classic sausage rolls 141
coconut
  lime and coconut friands 56
  raspberry coconut slice 24
coffee
  coffee and walnut cake 53
  icing 72
corn
  courgette and corn loaf 179
  ham and corn quiche 124
courgette and corn loaf 179
cream cheese filled banana bread 162
cream cheese frosting
  lemon 70
  maple 70
  marmalade 70
cupcakes
  apple ginger cakes with lemon icing 58
  blackberry swirl lemonade cupcakes 50
  peanut heaven cupcakes 76

D
date pudding, sticky with caramel sauce 75
devil's food cake 79
drizzle, toffee 50

E
easy cheesy leek quiche 123
éclairs, caramel 72

F
featherlight sponge 60
feta
  olive and feta rolls 185
  smashed avocado and feta flatbread 172
figs
  honey and fig tiramisu cake 88
fish
  smoked salmon and asparagus quiche 124
flatbreads, seeded 171
  prosciutto and melon 172
  red onion, pear and goat's cheese 172
  smashed avocado and feta 172
  tomato and mozzarella 172
Florentine biscotti 30
flourless chocolate cake 87
focaccia, rosemary and garlic 174
frangipane, almond 97
friands
  almond 55
  chocolate and hazelnut 56
  lemon curd 56
  lime and coconut 56
  passionfruit and lemon syrup cake 56
  plum 56
  raspberry and white chocolate 56
frostings
  blackberry swirl 50
  lemon cream cheese 70
  maple cream cheese 70
  marmalade cream cheese 70
  meringue 82
  rich chocolate 79
  ricotta ginger 70
  whipped milk choc peanut 76

G
galette, rhubarb 105
garlic
  garlicky pumpkin and feta quiches 136
  rosemary and garlic focaccia 174
ginger
  apple ginger cakes with lemon icing 58
  caramel ginger crunchies 17
  ricotta ginger frosting 70
gingerbread wreaths 32

goat's cheese
  capsicum and goat's cheese quiche 124
  tomato and goat's cheese tart with rice and seed crust 120

H
ham and corn quiche 124
hazelnuts
  chocolate and hazelnut friands 56
  freeform beetroot and hazelnut tart 112
  hazelnut and dark choc cookies 12
honey
  honey and fig tiramisu cake 88
  honey jumbles 22
hummingbird banana bread 162

I
icings and frostings
  blackberry swirl frosting 50
  buttercream 18
  chocolate buttercream 66
  chocolate glaze 46
  chocolate icing 80
  coffee icing 72
  lemon cream cheese frosting 70
  lemon icing 58
  maple cream cheese frosting 70
  marmalade cream cheese frosting 70
  meringue frosting 82
  rich chocolate frosting 79
  ricotta ginger frosting 70
  royal icing 32
  toffee drizzle 50
  vanilla bean icing 63
  whipped milk choc peanut frosting 76

K
kale
  quinoa and kale tart 126

L
lamb
  lamb and mushroom pies 152
  rogan josh lamb pie 146
lamingtons 80

leeks
    chicken and leek pie 132
lemon curd friands 56
lemon thyme salt sprinkle 144
lemons
    lemon and pistachios biscuits 36
    lemon curd friands 56
    lemon icing 58
    lemon tart 101
    passionfruit and lemon syrup cake 90
    passionfruit and lemon syrup cake friands
      56
    tangy lemon slice 27
lentil sausage rolls 143
lime and coconut friands 56
loaves
    courgette and corn loaf 179
    quinoa and seed cheese quick loaf 182
    spiced pumpkin snacking loaf 186

M
M&M's biscuits 36
marshmallow pavlova 64
melons
    prosciutto and melon seeded flatbread
      172
melting moments 18
meringue frosting 82
mini macadamia, pecan, and walnut pies 94
mozzarella
    tomato and mozzarella seeded flatbread
      172
muffins, spinach and three cheese 165
mushrooms
    chunky beef and mushroom pies 149
    lamb and mushroom pies 152

N
nectarine and almond tart 97
New York cheesecake 48
no-knead spelt and linseed bread 177
nuts
    almond frangipane 97
    chocolate and hazelnut friands 56
    chocolate truffle almond slice 38
    freeform beetroot and hazelnut tart
      112

hazelnut and dark choc cookies 12
lemon and pistachios biscuits 36
mini macadamia, pecan, and walnut pies
    94
    nectarine and almond tart 97
    pear, maple and cashew tarts 107
    pecan and cinnamon biscuits 36

O
oats and sultanas chocolate chip cookies
    12
olive and feta rolls 185
one-bowl chocolate velvet cake 46
onions
    caramelised 151
    red onion, pear and goat's cheese flatbread
      172
orange and poppyseed biscuits 36

P
palmiers, berry jam and vanilla 28
panforte, spicy 111
parmesan
    pumpkin and parmesan scones 168
passionfruit
    passionfruit and lemon syrup cake 90
    passionfruit and lemon syrup cake friands
      56
    raspberry and passionfruit mile-high layer
      cake 82
pavlova, marshmallow 64
peach and raspberry tarts 102
peanut heaven cupcakes 76
peanut butter
    peanut butter and raspberry banana bread
      162
    peanut butter cookies 40
    peanut butter cup cookies 12
pears
    pear, maple and cashew tarts 107
    red onion, pear and goat's cheese flatbread
      172
peas
    beef and pea triangles 131
pecans
    mini macadamia, pecan, and walnut pies
      94

pecan and cinnamon biscuits 36
pies
    beef and pea triangles 131
    butter chicken hand pies 129
    chicken and leek pie 132
    chunky beef and mushroom pies 149
    lamb and mushroom pies 152
    mince pies 108
    mini macadamia, pecan, and walnut pies
      94
    rogan josh lamb pie 146
pistachios
    lemon and pistachios biscuits 36
pizza scrolls 166
plum friands 56
poppyseeds
    orange and poppyseed biscuits 36
pork and apple sausage rolls 118
prosciutto and melon seeded flatbread
    172
pudding, sticky date with caramel sauce
    75
pumpkin
    pumpkin and feta quiches, garlicky 136
    pumpkin and parmesan scones 168
    spiced pumpkin snacking loaf 186

Q
quiches
    blue cheese 124
    capsicum and goat's cheese 124
    easy cheesy leek 123
    garlicky pumpkin and feta 136
    ham and corn 124
    smoked salmon and asparagus 124
quinoa and kale tart 126

R
raspberries
    peach and raspberry tarts 102
    peanut butter and raspberry banana bread
      162
    raspberry and passionfruit mile-high layer
      cake 82
    raspberry and white chocolate friands 56
    raspberry coconut slice 24
rhubarb galette 105

rich chocolate chip cookies 12
rich chocolate frosting 79
ricotta ginger frosting 70
roast vegetable filo tart 117
rogan josh lamb pie 146
rolls, olive and feta 185
rosemary and garlic focaccia 174
royal icing 32

S

salmon, smoked and asparagus quiche
124
salt sprinkle, lemon thyme 144
sauces
  caramel 75
  tomato 144
  yogurt mustard 144
sausage rolls
  classic 141
  lentil 143
  pork and apple 118
scones, pumpkin and parmesan 168
scrolls, pizza 166
seeds
  mixed seed sprinkle 144
  quinoa and seed cheese quick loaf 182
  seeded flatbreads 171
  spelt and linseed bread, no-knead 177
silver beet and cheese snails 134
slab cake, chocolate 66
slice-and-bake biscuits 35
slices
  chocolate caramel 21
  chocolate truffle almond 38
  raspberry coconut 24
  tangy lemon 27
smoked salmon and asparagus quiche
124
snails, silver beet and cheese 134
soda bread, dark chocolate cherry and walnut
158

spelt and linseed bread, no-knead 177
spiced pumpkin snacking loaf 186
spicy panforte 111
spinach and three cheese muffins 165
spring vegetable tart 138
sprinkle, mixed seed 144
sticky date pudding with caramel sauce
75
sultanas
  oats and sultanas chocolate chip cookies 12
sweet potato tarte tatin 151

T

tahini yogurt 138
tangy lemon slice 27
tarte tatin, sweet potato 151
tarts
  apple and brie 114
  freeform beetroot and hazelnut 112
  lemon 101
  nectarine and almond 97
  peach and raspberry 102
  pear, maple and cashew 107
  quinoa and kale 126
  rhubarb galette 105
  roast vegetable filo 117
  spring vegetable 138
  tomato and goat's cheese tart with rice
  and seed crust 120
toffee drizzle 50
tomato
  tomato and goat's cheese tart with rice
  and seed crust 120
  tomato and mozzarella seeded flatbread
  172
tomato sauce 144
triple chocolate chip cookies 12

V

vanilla bean
  berry jam and vanilla 28

vanilla bean cream 87
vanilla bean icing 63
vegetables
  roast vegetable filo tart 117
  spring vegetable tart 138

W

walnuts
  coffee and walnut cake 53
  dark chocolate cherry and walnut soda bread
  158
  mini macadamia, pecan, and walnut pies
  94
whipped milk choc peanut frosting 76
white chocolate
  raspberry and white chocolate friands 56
  white choc and macadamia cookies 12
wreaths, gingerbread 32

Y

yogurt
  tahini yogurt 138
  yogurt mustard sauce 144

Acknowledgments

DK would like to thank Sophia Young, Simone Aquilina, Amanda Chebatte, Georgia Moore, and Joe Revill for their assistance in making this book.
The Australian Women's Weekly Test Kitchen in Sydney, Australia has developed, tested and photographed the recipes in this book.

Photographer James Moffatt.
Stylists Olivia Blackmore , Kate Brown.
Photochefs Rebecca Lyall, Elizabeth Fiducia, Angela Devlin, Amal Webster, Tessa Immens, Nadia Fonoff, Carly Sophia Taylor, Ross Dobson.